A SOLID
foundation

Marriage
from
Three
Perspectives

E. Blake Scott & Melecia E. Scott

Largo, MD
USA

Christian Living Books
P. O. Box 7584
Largo, MD 20792
christianlivingbooks.com
We bring your dreams to fruition.

ISBN Paperback 9781562293147
ISBN Electronic Version 9781562293154

Printed in the United States of America

To Jesus – the Love of our lives

Solid Foundation
MARRIAGE MINISTRY

CONTENTS

INTRODUCTION

If you've been married for ten days, ten years or plan to get married in the future, it doesn't matter. This book will provide you with some of the tools you'll need to build a strong, healthy marriage. It is designed and written according to God's original blueprints for marriage and will greatly benefit both spouses.

Marriages are under attack; there is no doubt about it. The challenges have increased dramatically within the last five to ten years. Very often, couples wonder: "Are we the only ones going through this?" or "Why is this only happening in our marriage?" At times, they feel ashamed and unwilling to admit that there is a problem. Consequently, the marriage weakens – just like an old, abandoned house that's left to deteriorate.

Unfortunately, we are living in a time when people no longer take marriage covenants seriously. Some are signing divorce papers without giving a second thought. However, there are still some couples who have chosen to fight for their marriages. They are determined to build and rebuild them on a solid foundation. The question is "How will they succeed?" Wisdom and knowledge will get the work done.

In *A Solid Foundation*, we liken marriage to building a house from the ground up. We give you some of the necessary tools, tips, and plans to build a strong, healthy marriage beginning with a solid foundation. Husbands and wives will learn proven and effective building techniques that will strengthen their marriage and help to sustain it for a lifetime!

It's important to know that the foundation of a marriage is laid at the beginning stages. If the foundation is weak or unstable the marriage will be the same. The ambiguity of perspectives within all marriages can create stress, disappointment, and emotional upheavals. However, couples need to understand and accept the fact that in all marriages, there are three perspectives: God's, the husband's, and the wife's. Common ground must be reached before the next building phase can begin.

There is more to marriage than just the framework. It is inevitable that the builder will face problems when constructing a house. In many instances, difficulties are not discovered until the construction has begun. However, as challenging and frustrating as the project may be, good builders hardly ever back down or give up – they stick and stay.

A Solid Foundation aims to help married couples – or those who are contemplating marriage – do the same: "stick and stay" just like the mortar applied to each brick and every nail that has been hammered in a new house.

We strongly encourage both husbands and wives to read this book and learn how to apply the life lessons. We truly believe that it will be beneficial in building the marriage God has purposed and designed.

In life, sometimes you need to sharpen your tools before using them. Later, when they become dull again, you need to re-sharpen them. This book was written in hopes of sharpening up your old tools and when needed supplying you with new ones. It is no secret that marriages become dull at some point and just like your tools, they need to be re-sharpened.

Today, I hope you will decide on a marriage inspection, and let God, through this book, tear down the old and rebuild the new on a solid foundation.

CHAPTER 1

The Breaking

In marriage, a man and woman take a sacred vow to love, honor, and cherish each other until death. It is a solemn covenant. The two people become one flesh.

> That is why a man leaves his father and mother and is united to his wife, and they become one flesh. (Genesis 2:24)

As the bride and groom stand at the altar on their wedding day to commit themselves exclusively to each other, they do so in the very presence of God. The bride and the groom will also willingly accept that the marital covenant is a permanent and unending vow that binds couples together "until death." The wedding itself can be a time of mixed emotions. As we reflect on the vows, they resound within us causing us to deeply ponder if we are indeed ready to fully commit. Those of us who by faith have already said, "I do" understand why the bride and groom may be a bit nervous. We have a good idea why they are somewhat on-edge as they stand at the altar preparing to unite in holy matrimony.

Some people wait a long time for their wedding day. When it finally comes, it is, perhaps, one of the most glorious days they have experienced. Many times, it may even be the most eagerly anticipated day of their lifetime. Months of hard work and rigorous planning are put into this special day, and the couple prays that every "I" has been dotted and every "T" has been crossed. After the ceremonial pomp and circumstance, the actual repetition of the vows is done.

The bride and the groom stand at the altar ready to make a vow before God first, and secondly, to pledge their loyalty to each other. As the minister prepares to lay the foundation for the building, the couple looks intently at him. The man is asked: "Will you have this woman to be your wife?" "Will you make your promise to her in all love and honor, in all duty and service, in all faith and tenderness to live with her, and cherish her, according to the ordinance of God and in the holy bond of marriage?" A similar question is posed to the woman. With each spouse answering, "I will" or "I do," the two make a vow to each other. The minister will recite covenantal vows to both spouses requiring a response. Or, both spouses may choose to memorize and recite covenantal vows from their hearts.

I COVENANT WITH YOU!

Let us open our hearts and minds to envision this thrilling moment as the minister now asks the bride and the groom to face each other and to recite their vows as they stand at the altar. Face to face, they stare passionately into each other's eyes. Looking in amazement, the intensity of the moment creates an adrenaline rush that causes their hearts to beat simultaneously. As their hearts pound with excitement, their hands lock tightly, and they humbly vow their eternal love to each other.

However, the exchanging of vows is not the only special part of the wedding ceremony because as they pledge their love to each other, there is a change in the atmosphere. The Spirit of God pours out from Heaven and floods the sanctuary, saturating their souls, causing them both to be captivated by each other's presence. As tears flow down their cheeks, their emotions are stirred uninhibitedly; sweat protrudes between their fingers – the bride and the groom are totally immersed in the moment.

Every girl dreams about her wedding day. She envisions it as a perfect day when she is adorned majestically in the perfect wedding gown. It is her time to shine brightly and as radiant as the sun in all its beauty and splendor. Much detail and planning go into finding the ideal dress and all the beautiful accessories. Her shoes are perfect, and her makeup is flawlessly applied. She anticipates that the wedding party will be supportive and the sanctuary will be filled with the fragrance of beautiful, sweet flowers and candles, all in preparation for her to marry her earthly king. A Christian woman desires the glory of God to be upon her in this moment of honor. As she walks down the aisle to meet her groom, she hopes for a perfect day.

> *During the exchanging of vows, the Spirit of God pours out from Heaven and floods the sanctuary.*

She is a believer who has learned from the Bible and prayed for her steps to be ordered by God. Walking gracefully down the aisle, she smiles and looks toward Heaven placing her trust and her future in God's hands. She has used wisdom and chosen not to lean on her own understanding (Proverbs 3:5-6).

Underneath her veil rests her long flowing locks that have been swooped into a ponytail tucked into a classy bun lifted off her neck. Her stunning hairdo will later be revealed after her soon-to-be husband gently lifts her veil and seals the deal with a beautiful, awe-inspiring kiss. It is a momentous and holy occasion.

As the two of them recite their vows at the altar before God and witnesses, I can almost promise you that both the man and woman are doing so from two entirely different perspectives. Here are two individuals vowing to meet each other's needs. Do they understand what that means and what it looks like? Does the man understand the woman's most important need? Does the woman know what is the man's greatest need?

Willard F. Harley, Jr.'s book, *His Needs, Her Needs,* speaks a great deal about this subject. According to him, realistically, we know that all needs will not be met by our spouses. However, within this holy union, some things are exclusive and strictly reserved for holy matrimony. Both the man and woman expect their greatest needs to be satisfied by the other partner. What are those greatest needs?

The most significant need to be fulfilled from a man's perspective is his sexual need. And the most important need from a woman's perspective is affection. Yes, there are other desires within the marriage to be met but what is considered as a priority for one couple may not be a priority for the next. The list of needs varies from marriage to marriage.

FIRST THINGS FIRST

Healthy marriages require teamwork. They don't just happen. There has to be effort and hard work from each partner. As the saying goes, "Anything worth having is worth fighting for." Are you willing to work on your marriage? Are you willing to invest your time and energy to make your marriage strong? As born-again believers, our marriages are based on Christian principles. We choose to follow the guidelines and teachings established by God through Christ Jesus in the Bible.

> Therefore everyone who hears these words of mine and puts them into practice is like a wise man who built his house on the rock. (Matthew 7:24 NIV)

Marriages are built from the ground up just like houses. You first need a strong foundation, which is your faith in the Word of God and your relationship with Jesus Christ. Secondly, you need all the right tools to get the job done. Lastly, you need the wisdom to know which tools to use at the appropriate time.

Before you build, you first have to purchase the property or land from the owner. After that, you are given a title deed. This "legal paper" shows proof that the land/property has been purchased, and now it legally belongs to you. In turn, it gives you the legal right and clearance to start building your new home.

Men, now you are married, the woman legally belongs to you – she is yours. And ladies, legally, the man belongs to you – he is yours! When you purchase a piece of land, there is a legally binding contract between the seller and the buyer. But in marriage, the man and woman are bound together by a covenant. What is the difference between a contract and a covenant? A covenant is based on trust between parties. A contract is based on distrust. (You will read more about covenants in chapter nine.)

After receiving the deed, you need to find a builder, someone to construct your home. The same goes for your marriage. In the book of Hebrews, the apostle Paul wrote in chapter 11 verse 10 that Abraham was looking for a city whose builder and maker was God. Abraham had faith in God, fully trusting His plans even when he couldn't visualize them. Abraham continued to seek the Lord for direction so that His purpose and plans could be fulfilled. Likewise, in building our marriages today, we need to seek the master builder, the one who can create the masterpiece for which we are searching.

Many people have flawed ideas of what marriage is and what marriage should look like because they do not include the master builder. During the building process, Blake and I took the time to look at several drawings and prints of various houses. We read and browsed some books before we started building. We engaged in these activities hoping to get more knowledge and a better understanding of what was going on. But the books only showed the drawings from a one-dimensional perspective.

Similarly, people have a one-sided and one-dimensional view of marriage.

However, when you look at the three-dimensional drawings, the picture comes alive! As we tried to visualize our home, it wasn't until we saw the three-dimensional drawings that things became clear. We need to view marriage through the drawings of three perspectives: God's, the husband's, and the wife's. Only then will things become clearer.

I can vividly recall when God blessed Blake and me with the opportunity to buy a lot and possess the title deed. We were so excited! Every day, we drove past the site behaving like two kids waiting for Christmas Day to arrive. Sometimes, we would even pull the car over to the side of the road and gaze at the empty dirt-covered lot for long periods of time. There were a few times when we parked our car so we could get out and sit on the dirt in the open field envisioning the result. We were looking forward to "breaking ground." The very idea of a new home consumed our thoughts, both day and night.

That's exactly how marriages are in the beginning; everything is new, exciting, fresh, and creative. The momentum is flowing; adrenaline is pumping; love is in the air! In the early stages of marriage, even during the fearful and challenging times, couples seem to remain very eager and willing to try new things, especially on the night before the wedding and a short time after that. On this special night, we can be sure that their imaginations run wild as they dream, anticipate, and anxiously wait to "break ground," to consummate their marriage. After that, the foundation can be laid and their "marriage building process" can begin.

BREAKING GROUND IS ONLY THE BEGINNING

In the summer of 1998 with the help of God, Blake and I were finally able to possess the land and break ground on our property. It was truly a memorable moment as we sat and watched the construction crew drive down our street with all of the equipment on the flatbed truck. There were different types of trucks the crew brought in to assist them in plowing the dirt and digging deep trenches. This equipment allowed them to put the footers/beams in place to construct a strong and stable house. It was a very taxing but crucial process to ensure that we were building on a solid foundation.

In the New Testament, Jesus used parables of natural things to point out spiritual truths. In one of the parables, He talked about the heart, comparing it to soil or the ground.

> When anyone hears the message about the kingdom and does not understand it, the evil one comes and snatches away what was sown in their heart. This is the seed sown along the <u>path</u>. The seed falling on <u>rocky ground</u> refers to someone who hears the word and at once receives it with joy. But since they have no root, they last only a short time. When trouble or persecution comes because of the word, they quickly fall away. The seed falling among the <u>thorns</u> refers to someone who hears the word, but the worries of this life and the deceitfulness of wealth choke the word, making it unfruitful. But the seed falling on <u>good soil</u> refers to someone who hears the word and understands it. (Matthew 13:19-23 NIV)

Jesus spoke of four different types of soils and He emphasized the importance of breaking up the hard ground/soil so that seeds could be planted (take root) and bring forth fruit. The same applies to our marriages as we begin the building process.

It is important to humble ourselves and let God's Word and His Spirit humble us (softening the ground/our hearts). Humility allows God's Word to take root and in return, produce the spiritual fruit found in Galatians 5:22-23 – love, joy, peace, patience, goodness, kindness, gentleness, faithfulness, and self-control.

Believe it or not, this is a process of transformation as the power of God's Spirit rebuilds us from the inside out. However, be warned that this is a lifelong process. As humans, we will forever be under construction – going through the change process. If we continuously yield our hearts to the teachings of Christ and apply them to our marriages, our lives will be impacted. As a result, we will change the way we think, which inevitably changes our actions and how we respond. The Holy Spirit can empower us individually and collectively so that our marriages can mature and flourish in every area. The tools that are needed for tilling the ground of your hardened heart are repentance, forgiveness, and trust in God.

The desired result: humility. Build on humility and look for the best in your mate. It is true neither of you is perfect, but transformation is possible. With determination on both parts, you can become perfect for one another. Having a successful, healthy marriage is not based on perfection because no perfect marriage exists. However, building a loving, faith-filled marriage is possible. It will take both spouses being willing to humble themselves, seek forgiveness from each other and God, and walk daily in faith, trusting God completely. Keep allowing God's Word to dig out all the gravel and rocks in your heart to maintain a smooth foundation.

LOOK FOR THE BEST!

So before the Lord blessed us to build a house, we were blessed to buy one. During the time that Blake and I were engaged, he was deeply engrossed in real estate. Blake had a great passion for finding houses, fixing them up and transforming them into homes. No matter how bad the condition, Blake always had an eye for creativity. He saw great potential in some of the worst homes on the market. The very first home we purchased was to be a surprise and a gift for me. It was a fixer-upper – a HUD house – a home he bought very cheaply due to the extensive work and repairs that needed to be done on the inside. Excited and anxious to show me our new home, he called to set up a time to pick me up so he could drive me there to see it.

As we drove to the house, which was not very far from where we lived, our conversation was joyful and upbeat. He never mentioned anything about the condition or the appearance of the home to forewarn me. As we pulled up to the driveway, I smiled while at the same time nodding my head saying, "Yeah, this is really nice" as I looked around on the outside. However, as I stepped inside, my smile immediately changed to a frown, and my eyebrows turned in toward each other. I tell you, my whole facial expression was different as I walked in and saw the shell of this home.

I skimmed over the entire house within a few seconds, immediately noticing that some walls were missing while others needed to be torn down. The floor was piled with junk, and in the bathroom, someone had pulled up the toilet bowl and placed it inside the bathtub. I gazed with a perplexed look, thinking to myself, "hmmm OK."

Blake asked, "So what do you think?"

I responded, "It's nice!!" However, after he read my facial expressions, he said with excitement and confidence, "Yes! This is going to be our new house! After we put a little paint on some walls, fix and repair the others and purchase some carpet, it will look as good as new."

As he spoke, I was standing there looking at him like, "Oh! OK! If you say so."

"Yeah!" Blake said, "Just a few cosmetic makeovers and some TLC, and it will look like it's brand new again! It will be alright, Melecia! Don't worry."

And you know what? Blake was exactly right, a few months after, our home was refurbished – the end result was amazing! It looked beautiful; it was like brand new.

I used this example to show how God and our spouses see us. They get the bird's eye view. On the outside, we look good, maybe, even smell good, but only God and our spouses can really see the inside of us. They see (the real us behind closed doors) – the good, the bad, and the ugly. They see the broken walls, flaws, and imperfections. Even if we try to hide our true selves, we can only hide and mask our real identity temporarily. Eventually, the real us will be revealed. However, the good news is, just like that home I described, we too can be transformed in one way or another. The truth is, if we are honest with ourselves, we will admit that we can all use a little inside remodeling on our character, our attitudes, our speech, and our bad habits.

Even with all the negative traits we see in our spouses, it's still possible to find something good to say about them. Sometimes, we need to take another look at the individual from God's perspective. All I could see in that house was a little broken down "hut." But my fiancé chose to look with the eyes of faith. He saw a beautiful masterpiece in the making; he saw the good instead of focusing on the bad. God sees us, His children, from a totally different perspective.

Again, from my point of view that house was not fit for anyone to live in. I turned my nose up, and I was ready to walk the other way. In my opinion, it wasn't worth it. In some marriages, couples want to give up so easily when things don't "look good." Instead of staying and waiting it out, pressing through, enduring the process and allowing God to make our marriages the masterpiece He intended, we walk away. Keep in mind, when I use the word masterpiece, I am not referring to perfection.

True beauty is in the eyes of the beholder. There is a famous quote that says, "One man's trash is another man's treasure." God alone is the decider and judge of what's beautiful and what's not –not man. He instituted marriage, and He alone knows the reins of our hearts. God is the supreme builder and maker of all things. He knows exactly what we need to shape and mold us into the image of His Dear Son. He knows how to smooth out the rough patches in our lives. He knows when and where we need hammering (discipline). Because He is omniscient, He knows what's required in our marriages to bring down walls of hurt, pain, bitterness, jealousy, hatred, pride and the like. He also knows how and where to rebuild broken walls of self-love, loving others, low self-esteem, joy, peace, contentment, and forgiveness.

Let me reiterate, there are some specific needs we depend on our spouses to meet, but our spouses are not God. The majority of our needs can only be met and fulfilled by our Creator as we surrender ourselves to His workmanship. Then and only then can we achieve these desired results. Don't look to your spouse to fix you – he can't – she can't. The truth of the matter is, they can't even fix themselves completely; without God's help, we can do nothing.

The tool that is needed: truth. Jesus said, 'I am the Way, the Truth, the Life!' (John 14:6)

KEEP IT REAL

Facing the reality of who we are can sometimes be disheartening. Often, when we don't like what we see behind closed doors or in private, we become hesitant and/or unwilling to share that truth about ourselves with other people. For many, masking our hurt and pain is much easier to do than exposing it. Revealing something that is "ugly" requires courage to actually admit and to face the consequences.

King David in the Bible had the courage to pray and ask God to create a clean heart and renew the right spirit within him after he committed a great sin. His confession leads me to believe that David had a revelation of himself and as he discovered the truth, he had the conviction to pray and ask God to forgive him.

Without faith and trust in God to help us overcome whatever obstacle we may be facing, we will sink deeper and deeper under the weight of the problem. Then, we will slowly start wilting over into the pot of self-pity, guilt, and shame, which will weigh us down even more. It's not always easy to stand-up in the face of adversity, but God makes it clear that He is there to help. In life, we are all allowed to make choices. If we choose to rise above the criticisms, and judgments of others and ourselves, it is up to us. But with God as our anchor, we can rise above the raging sea and be afloat once again. Your marriage has hope, and that hope is in God alone.

Go to God in prayer! From here on, commit to building your marriage on truth! I'm not saying you have to go to your spouse and disclose your innermost dark secrets, no. The truth that I am speaking of is the truthfulness of God's Word. When your perspective is different from your spouse's, commit to looking at things from God's viewpoint. Allow Him to usher in peace; this is a part of building on the truth. A commitment to building on truth requires that both spouses have the correct view of themselves. The straight-up fact is, you are both imperfect. Neither the husband nor the wife always has the answer, and neither the husband nor the wife always knows what to do in every situation, but it's OK!

The fact may be that in your marriage, you are both experiencing many challenges right now, and you've both made some terrible choices. However, you may now realize that the biggest mistake you made was not consulting with God first. Even though it may not seem that way, many of our fiery tests come to teach us and generate growth and maturity. From God's perspective, we can view it as God purifying and refining us. The process of purification and refinement is similar to what happens with the materials and tools that are used to construct and build homes. These metals, before they become sturdy tools that help give our homes shape and strength are placed in the fire, pounded, hammered, scraped and molded – just like our marriages.

Blake and I have experienced many challenges, problems, frustrations, struggles, heartaches, tears, arguments, regrets, pains, sadness, grief…you name it. But we have also experienced many victories and joys! And all of the good, by far, outweighs the bad!

Each and every marriage is a work in progress, so don't ever feel like you're the only one suffering from marital issues. However, the perspective you have and the truth that you hold on to will greatly influence your outcome. Are you choosing to see the glass half empty or half full? God, through His Holy Spirit, wants to make adjustments in you both, if allowed. The truth is, it's not always her to blame for your lack of contentment, peace or joy; the truth is, it's not always him to blame. It's important to be honest with yourself about *you*; what changes do *you* need to make?

> For by the grace given me I say to every one of you: Do not think of yourself more highly than you ought, but rather think of yourself with sober judgment, in accordance with the faith God has distributed to each of you. (Romans 12:3)

The Bible also teaches that we all come short of God's glory and that there is none righteous (Romans 3:10). It's so easy to point out the mistakes of others, while never giving a thought about our own. I know I'm guilty of this; what about you?

HE LOVED ME THROUGH IT ALL

The validation of genuine love is so powerful. God's love is authentic, real, and true. His love is superior to that of anyone who has ever loved us and anyone who will ever try to love us. God's love is purely given and purely expressed. That means that through the evil of this world and our sinful flesh, there will always be efforts to make it to be totally opposite of God's original purpose and plans.

> The thief comes only to steal and kill and destroy; I have come that they may have life, and have it to the full. (John 10:10 NIV)

When you have never experienced genuine love, it's so easy to fall prey and pursue imitation love, a tainted love that's often used against others and takes advantage of them. In this day and time, everyone is seeking love and happiness. Some people do so through relationships, sex, wealth, success, pleasure, skills, power, pets or people. Everyone wants to be validated by love. When the link of real love is missing, it leaves a void, an emptiness, a longing, and an insatiable thirst that as humans, we set out on a mission to fill.

It doesn't matter if you're a man, woman, boy or girl, we can all identify with this longing because we all have it. We long to be accepted; we long to be valued; we long to be praised in some form or another. For example, a child may want love and praise for good grades, a mother for her tireless work around the house and a ministry worker may want recognition and appreciation for his or her faithful service to God and to the community. However, in the covenant of marriage, this standard holds even greater importance. It is crucial for husbands and wives to affirm and validate each other for the countless things that are done and the many sacrifices that are made on a daily basis.

Affirmation is like oxygen to our bodies – it's life! Without oxygen, we can't breathe or function properly. If our bodies lack oxygen long enough, we will die. Likewise, our marriages without affirmation will die. Affirmation is a must. It's a need and if it's not given within the marriage, the hunger for it could lead your spouse to seek it outside the marriage.

I can recall the day that I met Blake at his home. I was 17 years old, and I had just completed my junior year in high school. However, a few months before is *really* where it all began. It was a beautiful, yet, brisk summer day when I decided to go into a local Wendy's restaurant for lunch. As I entered the restaurant, I walked up to the cashier to order my food; she asked me if my order was to go or if I was eating in the restaurant. I replied, "To go." So, after a few minutes of waiting, the cashier politely handed me my food in a bag and said, "Have a nice day!" I replied, "Thank you, you too!"

After I had left the counter, I went over to the condiment bar to get ketchup and napkins, after which, I was prepared to exit the restaurant to continue my day. However, as I proceeded towards the exit door, I can vividly recall my eyes becoming as magnets being pulled and drawn in the direction of a very attractive man. Slowly, my head turned as I became captivated by his piercing and charming smile. I felt an instant connection – his heart with mine. While still walking, I continued to look over in his direction, staring at his muscular physique, smooth light brown complexion, his beautifully arched eyebrows, his perfectly trimmed mustache, and his lustrous black curly hair that was tapered on the sides. I thought, "Wow! That's a lot of man; he must be a body builder."

You see, at that time, I was a very frail young lady. I only weighed about 100 pounds, and I was a very skinny, insecure, and angry teenager. The thought of Blake ever being with someone like me was farfetched. I mean what could he possibly see in a knock-kneed, skinny girl like me? So after a few days of passing him in the restaurant and never saying a word, my mind was trapped in that moment of time. I just couldn't get him off my mind; I reminisced about him for days.

Finally, after not being able to shake the thought of him, I called Ayeesha, a good friend of mine to tell her about the incident. As we conversed on the phone, I described him the best way I could, explaining to her that he was possibly related to one of her track mates whom she ran with. Our city is very small and everybody knows everybody, so after the track state-ment, her memory was sparked and she exclaimed: "Oh yeah, I know him; I know the whole family; they are the Scotts!

I said, "Oh! OK! I would really like to meet him, girl."

"Yeah, no problem," Ayeesha said, "I know the whole family; his mom is cool, and I know where they live; we can go visit him this Friday after school."

"Really girl, this Friday?"

"Yeah!" responded Ayeesha.

So that Friday after school, which happened to be the last day of our junior year, we went to visit the man whom God had chosen to be my future husband.

After pulling up at his beautiful home, we got out of the car, approached the door, and rang the doorbell. Someone yelled from inside their house, "Who is it?"

Ayeesha, my friend responded, "It's Ayeesha."

A few minutes later, his mom politely opened the door.

"Hi Mrs. Scott," Ayeesha greeted.

"Hi Ayeesha," said his mom.

"Is Blake here?"

"Yes, Blake is here; you can come on in."

"Blake," his mom yelled, "There is someone at the door to see you."

Blake walked into the foyer and greeting us with a "Hello." Then, he invited us both into their family room. As we sat on their butter-smooth leather couch, Blake and Ayeesha began chatting. After a few minutes of talking and laughing, Ayeesha paused their conversation to introduce the two of us.

"Blake this is Melecia. Melecia this is Blake."

We both smiled, and from that point on, the two of them included me in the conversation. After we all conversed and laughed for a while, Ayeesha and I thanked Blake for inviting us in, and for being the sweet, kind-hearted person that he is. He thanked us both for coming. As we walked back to the front door, he asked me if he could take me out for dinner later. We exchanged numbers, went to dinner and the rest is history.

Who would have known that this day back in 1986, would begin a whole new chapter in my life? God strategically sent me to the man whom he had chosen for me. A man He knew would love me through it all, the good, the bad, and the ugly!

Our relationship started out quite smoothly. Blake's attitude and mannerisms towards me were regal, and he possessed such a spirit of humility and kindness, it was infectious.

As you can see, when I met Blake, I already had several insecurities, like most of us. I was insecure about my weight because I was often teased for being so skinny. In addition to that, I was suffering from mild acne, which later turned into severe acne, so I was ridiculed for my appearance. Secretly, I was struggling with many demons that I had opened myself to as a teenager. I was dealing with past relationships and hurts that weighed heavily on me. I'm sure you all can relate. It was a constant battle in my mind and in my spirit.

To be honest, at that time and many years after, I didn't even love myself because I didn't know how. I needed to face the "ugly" truth of who I was and that I was not who I was pretending to be. So, who was I after many years of having pieces of me taken? Who was I after being robbed of my integrity and identity? Who was I? Why was I so angry? Why was I so hateful? Why did I feel locked and imprisoned by my emotions? Why? And when did it all start? More importantly, did I need to have all the answers to my questions and problems before I could heal and move on?

In 2015, my dad died of pancreatic cancer. For years, he had been bothered by different symptoms: pains in his stomach, loss of appetite, chest pains, shoulder pains, you name it. He was dying slowly and didn't even know it. He could describe all the symptoms to a tee, and he was aware internally that something was wrong. However, in his stubbornness, he refused to go to the doctor, and he declined to seek help time and time again. It was not until he approached his fourth stage of cancer that he was diagnosed. It was around that same time that he and I had become extremely close. For many years, he would not go see a physician or get treatment of any kind for the ailments. However, the how's and why's of what caused the cancer were not predicated on his healing and a cure when he was diagnosed, he needed to yield to treatment.

Have you yielded yourself to treatment? Spiritual treatment? It is very likely that you're aware of the many symptoms that are causing your mental and emotional pain, just to name a few. Within yourself or maybe within your marriage, there are concerns and some issues. Like cancer, they seem to be spreading and becoming worse, but you're still refusing treatment.

> For the word of God is alive and active. Sharper than any double-edged sword, it penetrates even to dividing soul and spirit, joints and marrow; it judges the thoughts and attitudes of the heart. (Hebrews 4:12 NIV)

God's Word not only has the power to examine and diagnose us, but it also heals emotionally, mentally, spiritually, and physically – if you allow it.

My dad suffered from a lot of pain, some of which could have been minimized, avoided or better managed if he had only visited the doctor and sought treatment early. God is a great pain manager, and no problem is too big or too small for Him.

I am reminded of Jesus in the Bible, even when His burden became so heavy while carrying His cross, help was sent.

> Come to me, all you who are weary and burdened, and I will give you rest. Take my yoke upon you and learn from me, for I am gentle and humble in heart, and you will find rest for your souls. (Matthew 11:28-29)

Just like my dad was guilty of rejecting help and treatment, I too was guilty. A few months into our relationship, I began to reject Blake. I shutdown and withdrew from him, ignored his phones calls, and declined dates. For years, I had put my guard up and I was determined not to let him break through the walls of my heart. In hindsight, I realize that it wasn't necessary to have the answers to *all* my questions. I only needed to embrace the help and healing that was being sent. It only required one step to set things in motion.

How many times have we rejected the blessings of God because they didn't come packaged the way we anticipated? I am reminded of the story of the man who prayed for help, but every time God sent help to him, he turned it down because the help didn't look or come the way he had envisioned it. God sent me help; He sent me someone who would love me through it all, even though I didn't deserve it. You know what I mean? Even though we don't deserve Jesus' help and His love, He provides it over and over again, and He loves us through it all! Thank You, Lord!

From the time I met Blake, he has always been a perfect gentleman, and I wasn't accustomed to that. I grew up in the middle class, but I still had the "hood" in me. I wasn't used to any man doing nice things for me. I wasn't accustomed to being treated with great respect from men. So, I didn't know how to handle his love, attention, and respect. I had my guard up for months; I just could not bring myself to trust him. In the back of my mind, the thought lingered, "You are just too nice; what do you want from me? Uh!" Months into our relationship, my mother observed my consistently rude behavior towards him. She peacefully intervened and said, "Lisa, either you're going to be nice to that young man, or leave him alone. STOP being mean to him!" With that, I stopped being rude and gave him and our relationship a chance.

As our relationship progressed, we began spending countless hours together during spring break because Blake was a junior in college at Howard University. During his time home from college, we shared an enormous amount of time together hoping to know one another better. It was part of the building process before our marriage. During this period, I discovered that Blake was not a born-again believer. However, God used me to introduce him to Jesus Christ! Shortly after that, he was baptized.

God was teaching me, healing me, and lavishing His love on me through this man named Blake.

Paul paints a picture of what love really is:

> Love is patient, love is kind. It does not envy, it does not boast, it is not proud. It does not dishonor others, it is not self-seeking, it is not easily angered, it keeps no record of wrongs. Love does not delight in evil but rejoices with the truth. It always protects, always trusts, always hopes, always perseveres. Love never fails. But where there are prophecies, they will cease; where there are tongues, they will be stilled; where there is knowledge, it will pass away. For we know in part and we prophesy in part, but when completeness comes, what is in part disappears. When I was a child, I talked like a child, I thought like a child, I reasoned like a child. When I became a man, I put the ways of childhood behind me. For now we see only a reflection as in a mirror; then we shall see face to face. Now I know in part; then I shall know fully, even as I am fully known. And now these three remain: faith, hope and love. But the greatest of these is love. (1 Corinthians 13:4-13 NIV)

Artificial love is the total opposite of the above biblical love. Imitation love has no problem smiling in your face while it's plotting and scheming behind your back. This fake, hypocritical love schemes and plots viciously. The Bible says that Satan, himself, masquerades as an angel of light (2 Corinthians 11:14). He strives to distort the gospel of truth and the ways of God. The same is true of disingenuous, artificial love; this masked love has goals that are to selfishly gratify its own desires. This kind of "love" is a substitute that temporarily fills us up. It is like a high that soon wears off. It's that thrill of getting something new then, in a few days, the thrill is gone.

Sometimes, we tolerate and accept love in many different forms (real or not) because of our need to be loved. Unfortunately, our past hurts and pains can leave us feeling that any kind of love is better than no love at all. So out of anger, hurt, impatience, greed or frustration, we become vulnerable to this masked love that later leaves its residue on us, making us feel even worse than when we first got involved. For example, when someone says "I have fallen out of love with you" or "I just don't love you anymore." According to the Bible, "unconditional" love does not seek its own, that's a superficial kind of love. It's a love that seeks only to please itself, not others. It is entirely opposite to the love that the apostle Paul described in 1 Corinthians chapter 13.

A marriage with a solid foundation of real love can only be constructed by God. No other supplier has this authentic material. Build on the Word of God! Build on healing and build on love!

SIX TYPES OF LOVE IN THE GREEK

Eros – Represents the idea of sexual passion and desire.

Philia – Friendship that develops brotherly love.

Ludus – Playful love, which refers to the affection between children and young lovers. Flirting and teasing in the early stages of a relationship.

Agape – A selfless love, a love that you extend to all people, whether family or distant strangers.

Pragma – Mature love, the deep understanding that is developed between long-married couples. Making compromises to help the relationship work over time.

Storge – A wide-ranging force, which can be applied to family members, friends, pets, companions or colleagues. Family love, the bond among mothers, fathers, sisters and brothers.

CHAPTER 2
Pray Watch Work

It has been said, "There are three kinds of people in the world – those who don't know what's happening, those who watch what's happening, and those who make things happen." In one of the Old Testament books, we discover a man of great influence by the name of Nehemiah who made things happen. God gave him a burden regarding the conditions in Jerusalem. Do you have a burden for the condition of your marriage? Are you ready to see change? More importantly, are you ready to make changes?

What's so amazing about Nehemiah is that he chose not to ignore the burden. Often, that's what we tend to do. On many occasions, God places a burden on us to do something, fear grips us, and we try to escape it. But this is not the testimony of Nehemiah. He willingly shared in the burden that was placed upon him. He cared enough to do something so that he could help the Jewish people.

When God instructs you to do something, don't try to escape it, you may miss your blessing. What did God want Nehemiah to do? What was the burden? The burden was for Nehemiah to go and rebuild the walls in Jerusalem. For many years, the city was left in ruins, with burned gates and broken down walls. It was exposed to attacks from the enemy and looked upon as defenseless. In Nehemiah's time, rebuilding the walls and setting up the gates meant protection and security for the people of Jerusalem.

Today, the walls of many marriages have broken down, and the gates have been burned. They are being attacked and invaded by Satan, the world, and the flesh. Over the years, couples have become accustomed to or contented with the "ruined" conditions, possibly feeling there is nothing more they can do. But there is. You can rebuild the walls just like Nehemiah did. Will you accept that challenge? Will you respond like the people did and declare, "Let us rise up and build!"

I understand that this is a big task. Maybe you're experiencing some conflicting emotions right now because you've already tried to work on your marriage unsuccessfully. So why continue trying? Well, that's exactly what happened in Jerusalem years ago. The Jewish people had attempted to repair the walls before, but they were stopped! However, on the second attempt, they were successful. I implore you; don't be discouraged if you have tried numerous times already. If you're still eager and willing to keep trying, please, don't stop.

Recently, God sent a married couple to us; a couple experiencing many problems and challenges within their marriage. We were given the opportunity to be a listening ear and to offer them wise counsel from the Word of God. God gave us a burden for someone else's broken down walls.

After conversing over the phone for a few minutes, we decided that it would be best they came over to our house so that we could talk face to face. We had no problem with that. They arrived at our home, we invited them inside and immediately asked if we could all pray. When they agreed, we bowed our heads and closed our eyes as we petitioned the Lord for wisdom, inviting Him to come into our midst so the building process could begin.

CARE ENOUGH TO DO SOMETHING

Let's take a look at Nehemiah's prayer:

Nehemiah cared enough to do something; do you? Now that you have been given a burden for the broken walls in your marriage, how do you plan to prepare for the rebuilding process? Which tools are you planning to use? Well, some of the tools that Nehemiah used to help him get started were prayer and fasting! Nehemiah immediately realized that he could not do the work alone, he needed God.

> When I heard these things, I sat down and wept. For some days I mourned and fasted and prayed before the God of Heaven. Then I said: "LORD, the God of Heaven, the great and awesome God, who keeps his covenant of love with those who love him and keep his commandments, let your ear be attentive and your eyes open to hear the prayer your servant is praying before you day and night for your servants, the people of Israel. I confess the sins we Israelites, including myself and my father's family, have committed against you. (Nehemiah 1:4-6 NIV)

Tools to use as you begin rebuilding your marriage are faith, prayer, communication and fasting.

> *Accept the challenge and respond by saying, "Let us rise up and build!"*

CHAPTER 3

It's Time to Build

I n chapter one, the foundation was laid as we broke ground on our new property. In chapter two, we were encouraged to start the building process because rebuilding the walls would provide us with security and protection for our marriage. Here, in chapter three, we will actually start building. Are you ready?

It is imperative in any building project to follow a blueprint so that you can know the correct layout, design, and plan of action; building a marriage is no different. Have you ever tried to put something together without the instructions? You tried over and over again, but you just couldn't figure it out. You may have Googled how to assemble it or called someone to help you, but none of your efforts were successful. It caused you to become frustrated and dismayed, totally worn out from the many attempts. You shook your head, scratched the back of your neck and in utter disbelief you thought: "What in the world am I going to do? I've struggled with this thing all week long, and I haven't made any progress." You might have even slammed your hand down on the table.

"I. Am. So. Frustrated! For the life of me, I just cannot figure this out!" Just when you were about to give up trying, your eyes gazed upward and on top of the kitchen cabinet, lay the instructions. They were right where you left them. You thought you didn't need them; you could sort it all out on your own. So you put them there with the intention of throwing them away later.

How many of us have tried to do it on our own? How many times have we disregarded God's instructions? We felt we didn't need His guidance and help. Instead, we decided to just Google the problem or buy self-help books. How often do we neglect to get instructions from God and from His Word?

God is the Master Architect, the Master Builder, Master Designer, and the CEO of marriage. He provided us with the blueprints in His Word. But have we misplaced the instruction manual? What or who convinced us that we could do it on our own? Nevertheless, because of our choices, we are frustrated, ready to give up and throw in the towel. Perhaps, we are unable to figure out this marriage stuff! Dismayed, we walk around "scratching our heads" and wondering what to do.

STEPS IN BRICK LAYING

1. **The Foundation** – I can recall when the bricklayers started to build the basement block walls of our home. The master mason had to lay the first block. That first block is known as the cornerstone, which is the most crucial block that has to be laid. It must have taken the brick layers two hours to place that one block. I can remember asking Kenny, the master mason, why it was taking him so long to lay that one block. He told me that it was the cornerstone. If that one stone wasn't perfectly squared both horizontally and vertically, it would make EVERYTHING that was built upon it wrong and out of square. Jesus said: "I AM the chief cornerstone." If we're not building on Him, everything – including our marriages – will be out of square or unbalanced. We will be building a mess. After setting the cornerstone, the masons mixed mortar and went through the process of building the blocks with some being adjacent to each other while others

were staggered. Rome wasn't constructed in a day, they say, neither is the process of building a strong marriage. It takes work. It takes some hard work.

> *God is the Master architect, Master builder, Master designer, and CEO of marriage.*

2. **The Right Bricks** – As I watched the men building the block walls of the basement and sweating profusely, I thought, "That's strenuous work." Marriage is similar. It's not always going to be easy. Sometimes, you will have to say, "I'm sorry" even when you think you are right. You will have to sacrifice time, money, and resources. But these are things that Jesus did on our behalf. You have to lay bricks of forgiveness, patience, kindness, commitment, and sacrifice each and every day of your marriage. Laying bricks of forgiveness is a requirement of God. Jesus said: "We must forgive others that we too might be forgiven." I believe that sometimes, we forget the abundance of forgiveness that God has so graciously given to us. He forgives all of our wrongdoings when we go to Him in prayer. It is critical to remember that marriages are not mistake proof. We will make mistakes because we are human and as humans, we are destined to err. Having a realistic understanding of this leaves no room for holding grudges. Grudges are like cancer; they tend to eat away at our relationships with God and with each other. Harboring unforgiveness will only hinder the building progress. Have there been times that you didn't speak to your spouse for days? We are all guilty of doing this at one time or another.

But, the Bible instructs us in Ephesians 5:27, not to let the sun go down on our wrath. Harboring unforgiveness will truly do more harm than good.

3. **The Right Materials** – God has provided us with many resources – His Word being the most important. It is our blueprint and instruction manual on how to have a healthy marriage. He has also sent you this book along with many other God-inspired messages from other authors. Christian counseling is also available. Many churches provide counseling, either with the pastor of that church or a marriage ministry leader. Just keep in mind – building a home costs, and so does building a marriage.

4. **The Right Tools** – You've heard the expression "the right tool for the job" haven't you? Bricklaying tools include a mixer, wall ties, a bricklaying trowel, a spacing rule, and a level. However, the right tools for this job are, of course, your Bible, the Holy Spirit, prayer, Spirit led fasting, wisdom from God, time, patience, and sacrifice.

5. **The Right Plans** – Let's face it, without the right plans, you just won't be very successful. Your instruction manual, the Bible, contains the right plans for your marriage and will benefit you greatly. Be sure that your plans line-up with God's.

6. **Training** – The best person to help teach and guide you on the right path is the Holy Spirit; He is a great teacher. There are also pastors, leaders, and mentors available in local churches and in the body of Christ who are anointed to disciple others as well as to provide marital training.

7. **Practice** – After putting everything else in place, practice. Do it over and over and over again. Even if you make a mistake, which you will, it's imperative for the both of you to keep on trying. Stick to it!

CHAPTER 4

Order in Creation

A good builder determines the order of work before the building process starts. The inside is not drywalled until the walls are framed. Then, electrical wiring and plumbing are done according to the builder's blueprints. When the process is completed, everything comes together as the architect designed it to be. It is the builder's responsibility to schedule the work and employ the relevant tradesmen to build the house so that it comes together as planned. The same goes for God's creation and in our marriages.

Our awesome and mighty God is a God of order. Everything He does is well done. In the book of Genesis, we are provided with a vivid picture of the Creator at work. He unleashed the power of His words into the stratosphere of Earth and below, fulfilling every intended plan and purpose. We read as our awe-inspiring God commands light to separate from darkness by His authoritative speech on the first day, calling them "day" and "night."

On the second day, God created the firmament known as heaven (sky), placing waters above and below the firmament. The third day encompassed the creation of land and vegetation as God put land in the midst of the lower waters and called it "Earth." He called the waters "seas." God created every tree and plant according to its own kind and made them bear their own seeds.

On the fourth day, God made the sun, moon, and stars.

On the fifth day, God filled the ocean with sea animals and the heavens with birds.

On the sixth day, God created the land animals and then made man in His own image. Chapter two of Genesis explains that God let Adam, the first man, assign names to every other creature. And on the seventh day, God completed His work and then He rested.

And as we continue to read Genesis chapter two, we find that God caused a deep sleep to come over the man. As he slept, God took one of his ribs and closed the man's flesh. Then the Lord God made the rib He had taken from the man into a woman and brought her to the man. And the man said: "This is bone of my bone, and flesh of my flesh; this one will be called woman because she was taken from man." This is why a man leaves his father and mother and bonds with his wife, and they become one flesh. God has provided order in creation, and God has also provided order within the marriage.

ORDER IN MARRIAGE

Paul states:

> Submit to one another out of reverence for Christ. Wives, submit to your husbands as to the Lord. For the husband is head of the wife, just as Christ is the head of the church, His body, of which He is the Savior. Now as the church submits to Christ, so also wives should submit to their husbands in everything for the husband is the head of the wife as Christ is the head of the church, his body, of which he is the Savior. (Ephesians 5:21-25)

Paul also states that husbands are to love their wives as Christ loved the church and gave Himself up for her.

Often, women are reluctant to hearing this particular scripture. However, when you clearly understand its context, with the correct underlying principles, it makes it somewhat of an easier pill to swallow. This particular scripture that has been given to us by our loving heavenly Father contains the same teachings and principles that were applied and carried out by our Lord and Savior Jesus Christ.

During Jesus' earthly ministry, He stated: "My will is to do that of the Father." So, Jesus willingly accepted the duty and call of submission as He surrendered Himself to the plans and will of God. As women, we too have been given a call; it is to willingly submit ourselves to our husbands. This is the plan and will of God, just as it is for our husbands to love us as Christ loved the church and gave Himself up for her.

> *God has provided order in creation and also within marriage.*

FROM MY PERSPECTIVE AS A WIFE

God has blessed me with a very humble, loving, and caring husband. And because of his godly character, the call to submit to him as he submits and follows Christ has not been a difficult task for me. I can honestly say that in all of our twenty-five years of marriage, he has always approached me respectfully even at times when he had to be firm in suggesting that I not do something. His approach has made it easy for me to submit to him out of the same mutual love and respect that is shown to me.

FROM MY PERSPECTIVE AS A HUSBAND

Build your marriage on respect for each other!

Men, God can work on your spouse like none other. I can vividly recall when Melecia and I first got married; the challenges that we faced seemed insurmountable. At times, my wife was very impatient and very easily angered. However, today, I come to you with a different testimony of the amazing works of God. I'm here to tell you what He can do when there's order in your marriage and in both you and your spouse's relationship with God. The majority of the time, the only faults we can see are those in someone else. But I want to share with you that God has done a 180-degree turn in my wife's life. She is more loving, kind, and compassionate – just to name a few fruits of the spirit. My point is this: when things began to take order in our lives, it made us more loving toward God and one another. Thank God for His promises. Are things in order in your marriage? If not, it's time to seek God and ask Him to help you to put things in order.

ORDER IN THE FAMILY

So, God has a divine order for doing things – creation, the world, man and woman, husbands and wives, and even for family. There have been many times when Blake and I have struggled in this area of "order in the family." For me, the struggle became real as I totally embraced the call to ministry and began to immerse myself in it fully. After years of being a stay-at-home mom, I often contemplated finding a part-time job. I wanted to occupy some of my time while my children were at school, and I desired a sense of "independence." I had worked for many years before and after I was married. However, my husband gave me the option to "retire" from my hotel receptionist job at the age of 23, so I gladly accepted the offer.

However, after a few years passed, I really missed not working outside the home. So I told Blake I had a pressing desire to work again, and I was planning to seek employment. I did not realize that my son was listening to me as I made this comment to my husband. I can clearly recall my son Brendon, who was nine-years old at that time, saying, "Mom, please don't get a job and leave us here, stay home with us Mom, please!!!! Don't get a job!!" He was almost in tears as he spoke those words. My heart melted, and I responded: "OK son, Mommy is not going to leave you. Don't worry, I will stay home with you." Taking a deep breath and shaking my head, I looked towards Heaven and said, "OK Lord, I hear You." The reason I had responded to the Lord that way was that, deep down in my heart, I already knew what God wanted, but I wanted something different. I wanted a job outside the home. I wasn't fully content with being a stay-at-home mom; I felt what I was doing wasn't as important as what others were doing. You know how as women we tend to compare ourselves and our careers with others. At that time, I just wasn't contented, and I didn't feel validated by other people. Don't misunderstand me, I know there is totally nothing wrong with women working outside the home. But for me, God had other plans. Those plans required me to sit at His feet, do a lot of praying, studying, and reading so that I could prepare for my future calling in ministry.

I said, "Yes" to the Lord, threw out my plans of looking for a job and began the building process for my future ministry. Daily studying, praying, and reading while my children were in school were what God used to start my preparation for kingdom work. My husband and I both grew in our commitment to the Lord, and spiritual doors began to open. He was ordained as a deacon, and five years later, he was ordained as a minister.

For me, my greatest leap of spiritual promotion was when God led me to establish our Deaf Ministry. Within a few months after being placed in this leadership position, I became engrossed in the thought and act of being used by God. I had decided there was nothing more important to me than to please my God, and to do it with excellence. So, I totally plunged myself into serving God and others, allowing the work of ministry to fully consume me. For months, I unconsciously neglected my spouse and children, allowing my "business" to push them out of first place, which in return created disorder. At that time, I didn't quite know how to balance being a wife, a mother to four small children (I was also raising my nephew), being a homemaker and a ministry leader all at the same time. My priorities lost order, and I began to lose sight of my marriage and children.

As my husband became frustrated with me, I became more frustrated with myself. The disorder of my priorities had begun to weigh heavily on my marriage. My children began to despise Mommy working in ministry. They felt: "I hate having to share my mommy with so many people. She always puts us last." They automatically knew they had to wait or not to bother Mommy because she must put others (ministry) first. This was out of order!

However, let me be clear, my love for God was in order, but my purpose for ministry wasn't. Sometimes, we can start out with pure motives and intentions to do something, but because we are still in the flesh and struggle with pride, our focus and reasons for doing things can shift and change. I believe that as I began to rejoice that God was using me, feeling a sense of "worth" that I was now "working" and because I had something to validate me, my focus shifted, and ministry was more about the "work" and me than God.

I was out of order; my relationship with God was out of order; my marriage was out of order; my family was out of order. Not that we didn't love Him or that God wasn't using us, because He was. However, we were not experiencing the joy and peace of God as we could have because of our disobedience. Do you see how it's a trickling effect? Our family's foundation was shaky, for a season. I wasn't building on Christ; I started to build on selfish motives.

My husband's struggle became real as he began immersing himself in work and personal relationships that he put before me.

God's Word in Proverbs 22:6 teaches us to train our children in the way they should go. However, if I'm too busy to train and teach my children, I could be neglecting them emotionally, spiritually, and socially. We often see or hear on the news how children are being neglected or abandoned. We wonder how could people physically neglect their children. However, the same principle can apply to the child's emotions. As a parent, I am responsible for meeting the basic physical needs of my children as well as their emotional needs. God has entrusted me to fulfill one of the greatest responsibilities there is, and He didn't leave me clueless.

In fulfilling the plans of parenting, I often heard, "Children don't come with instructions." From the perspective of the world that holds true. However, from the viewpoint of a Christian, God left us the greatest instruction manual there is – the Bible. Through the Word of God, we are given instructions for everyday living.

We are admonished to teach our children godly principles at home. It's not the responsibility of the schools, the internet, churches, or even other family members to train them; it is the responsibility of the parents. God values family, and we should too. Ministry begins at home first then it extends to others. The love of God was first demonstrated through His Son and subsequently to others. As we look at the Father and the Son, we can see a picture of the family. God the Father loves and cherishes His Son, and Jesus the Son loves and honors His Father. In collaboration with the Holy Spirit, They all work together as one, ministering and working through the hearts of multitudes to establish order in the church.

ORDER IN THE CHURCH

Yes, God has established an order for His church, the body of Christ. As born-again believers, we have been given the title "Christians." Therefore, we have been charged to submit ourselves to the authority and headship of our Lord and Savior, Jesus Christ, so that we may glorify our Father in Heaven.

God as Creator, made the heavens and the earth; He also made man and woman whom He joined together as husband and wife – instituting the very first marriage. This holy union that God established in the garden is a divine pictorial of Christ and the church, "His bride." So how did God do this? He did all this in His infinite wisdom and might. God's systematic plan to redeem mankind to Himself was strategically laid out through a divine order of events. Our Sovereign God planned the immaculate birth of our precious Savior so that one day, He could be sacrificed for the sins of all. God willingly sacrificed His one and only Son Jesus for a lost and dying world.

> God so loved the world that he gave his one and only Son, that whoever believes in him shall not perish but have eternal life. (John 3:16 NIV)

God's plan was to emphatically provide hope for the hopeless. It was this divine plan that privileged us to be adopted into His royal family becoming heirs of God and joint-heirs with Christ. Yes, through Jesus, God provided us with hope for the here and now, as well as for the hereafter. Our triune God has so wondrously designed the plan of salvation through Jesus Christ. John 14:6 reaffirms this truth as it declares, "I am the way, the truth, and the life, the only way to the Father is through the Son."

God loves order; He established it from the beginning of time. Our heavenly Father has a specific way of doing things. This leads me to my next statement. If one is not adhering to or following God's plans and order, it simply means that things are being done out of order.

Now, we have established the importance of order when constructing a home and in building strong marriages. We would now like to draw your attention to a small but very powerful tool. During the early stages, builders use a level. A level is a tool used to ensure that each and every brick is centered and straight after it has been set in place. Levels are also used to make sure that the bricks are aligned correctly. Leveling is only a small part of this big task and can be easily overlooked or forgotten. However, it is a very important step. Likewise with our marriages, sometimes we tend to forget the little things that are very important. To help us keep things leveled and on track as we build it's crucial to pay attention to those.

DON'T FORGET THE LITTLE THINGS

1. "You look beautiful." "Thank you, so do you!" Complimenting one another is crucial.

2. When your husband takes the initiative to do something around the house or when he arrives home and notices something that you have done, it's important to give praise. Say, "Oh, I see you vacuumed the floor" or acknowledge whatever the person did in some way, including a nice comment.

3. "Thank you for dinner, it was delicious!"

4. As women, it's important for us to thank our spouses for being excellent providers, fathers, husbands, etc. and not just on Father's Day. On any given day, a kiss or a hug to just say thank you for being a great provider is worth more than you think.

5. Compliment your spouse for doing a good job in ministry or in the work place. You should be each other's greatest

cheerleader. Ascribe glory to God but still praise each other for being instruments used by Him.

6. Send personal text messages, encouraging quotes, an image of yourself (selfie) or leave voice mails just to say I love you or I'm thinking about you.

7. Clear your schedule for one on one time with each other.

8. Have weekend dates or getaways.

9. Make breakfast in bed before going to work or go out to breakfast before the work day begins.

10. Take them lunch on the job.

11. Pray together.

12. Massage each other or give a simple back rub with many kisses, saying thank you!

13. Have spontaneous dates.

14. Send flowers or a card just because.

15. Men, if you have a little time, join your wife while she's doing grocery shopping.

16. Women, join your husband while he's watching his favorite sport or TV program.

17. Take baths or showers together.

18. Take time to communicate with each other.

19. Have family time, games nights, include the kids and talk about future goals with them. Everyone can sit together and take turns saying something encouraging about each family member.

20. Allow each other space when needed.

CHAPTER 5

The Search

Everybody is looking for love. We all want to feel like we are loved and valued by others. In the smooth, soulful words of the late Marvin Gaye 1970s' hit song, "What's Going On?" Marvin wrote lyrics that pierced the hearts of many. This phenomenal writer wrote and sang about many relatable, painful, personal, heart gripping experiences. He was a musical genius who wrote many songs and messages about love and the lack thereof. He racked up millions of dollars in sales on various hit songs, and one of his best-selling records still rings true.

As you listen to the lyrics of "What's Going On," the title itself is presented to us in rhetorical form as Marvin offers the solution of love to the question that he repeatedly sings about. I'm sure you will agree with me that it speaks volumes on many issues that are still happening today. If you would, go back with me to around 1971, and listen to Marvin's album. You can't help but to immerse yourself in his lyrics and be moved by the rhythm of this jazzy beat, nodding to the powerful messages that speak volumes to those who choose to hear.

This mountainous smooth tune of jazz reverberates the very core of your soul causing your heart to connect to the lyrics and your mind to drift as the mellowness of the music brings calmness to your soul. The unique sound and instruments of this tune bounce off your shoulders as you sway from side to side connecting with this positive message. Feeling the beat of the drums vibrate from the speakers, you lock in and listen attentively as he addresses many heart-wrenching issues prevalent at that time.

His lyrics paint pictures of crying mothers, senseless killings amongst brothers as well as a lack of unity. This prolific writer proposes messages of peace, not of war to the fathers. He then transitions with a smooth melodious tune of equality, not forgetting to mention non-violence, racial discrimination and unfair judgment of others. Marvin's solution is to add love to the equation. He sends the message of exchanging hate for love and war for peace, foolishness for wisdom, ignorance for knowledge and open communication to hard-heartedness. So yes, in the words of our once-upon-a-time popular R&B hit song, tell me, "What's Going On?"

What's Going On

Mother, mother
There's too many of you crying
Brother, brother, brother
There's far too many of you dying
You know we've got to find a way
To bring some lovin' here today

Father, father
This don't need to escalate
You see, war is not the answer
For only love can conquer hate
You know we've got to find a way
To bring some lovin' here today

Picket lines and picket signs
Don't punish me with brutality
Talk to me, so you can see
Oh, what's going on?

What's going on?
What's going on, yeah?
What's going on?

Mother, mother
Everybody thinks we're wrong
Who are they to judge us
Just because our hair is long
You know we've got to find a way
To bring some understanding here today

You know we've got to find a way
To bring some lovin' here today
Picket lines and picket signs
Don't punish me with brutality
But just talk to me
So you can see
What's going on
Tell me what's going on
What's going on?
You tell me, I'll tell you
You tell me, I'll tell you what's going on

Songwriters: Alfred W. Cleveland, Marvin P. Gaye, Renaldo Benson
© Sony/ATV Music Publishing LLC

> *What's going on with love
> and unity within
> our families?*

It appears that Marvin Gaye had somewhat of a spiritual revelation on the will and purpose of God pertaining to our love walk. He voiced his concerns through his lyrics. Likewise, God expresses His thoughts; He speaks; He shares His heart with us through

His Word. When the Lord presents us with a question, it's not as if He doesn't already know the answer. God is omniscient; He knows all.

Today, we use the lyrics of this song to bring home our point. My mind goes back to Genesis when God spoke in the same tone and rhetoric to Adam in the garden in the cool of the day. He spoke from His heart, voiced His concerns for Adam and asked, "Adam where art thou?"

The same question can apply to each of us today. As a child of God, we can hear our loving Heavenly Father calling out to us from the pages of the bible saying, "Where art thou"? Where are you my child? I desire for you to know the truth. I desire to commune and fellowship with you, daily, just like I did with Adam. It is My desire to teach you and empower you with wisdom in the midst of everything that's going on in your marriage, and otherwise. Many of you have strayed away from me in your hearts, and my question to you today is, where are you?"

Marvin Gaye suggested that we find a way to bring back love. However, according to the scripture, the way has already been made, Jesus Himself says, "I am the way." (John 14:6) He also said, "apart from me you can do nothing." (John 15:5)

Yes, there is definitely a lot going on in the world. But to be honest, there is not a lot going on with this word we call "love" according to the Word of God. Love is a word that is used quite frequently. We have even created emojis to help us express our thoughts of love. Abbreviations are used and sometimes, we even shorten the word by using syllables; you name it. But all in all, love is a simple four letter word that seems to be so complicated. If we were to be honest with ourselves, we would admit that most of us just don't appear to understand it.

Tina Turner asked a question: "What's Love Got to Do with It?" Well, dear readers, love has everything to do with it! In our world today, we have millions of people writing, singing, and rapping about love, our ever so popular cupid shuffle dance has people "stepping" in the name of love. Over in the Middle East, many innocent people are dying and being slaughtered in the name of love. The mindset and perspective of our children today is that much stuff equals much love. If I don't have as much stuff as my friends and school mates – I'm not loved as much.

The music genres are so diverse today; our music choices are endless. There is gospel music, country music, hard rock, rap, classical, heavy metal as well as many popular R&B love songs that have very impactful messages to stir our emotions and energize our passions. Music has the ability to take our minds captive and center them on whatever is being sung or spoken at that time. The majority of songs give voice to and create mental pictures and images of that powerful word we call "love." Our television shows, commercials, books, magazines, and the internet are inundated with views and perspectives on romance, relationships, sex, and love.

The book of Hosea, chapter 4 reveals that God spoke through His prophet Hosea to the people of Israel. God chided the Israelites for being unfaithful and disloyal. They had drifted far away from Him. So the message He sent was, "My people are destroyed for lack of knowledge." As a matter of fact, verse 6 also says that they actually rejected knowledge.

Have we taken the time to gain a greater understanding of something so powerful? Or… have we only skimmed the surface of this word *love*?

According to online dating data, the search for love has hit an all-time high with many people on a quest to find it. This love search is evident through statistics that show an increase of members on online dating sites over the past 20 years. The first online dating service, Matchmakers (www.match.com), was created in 1995. Matchmakers reported millions registered as members for the year 2002. The same applies to Google match-maker where you will get thousands of results for that specific search. Today's statistics show that about 40 million Americans use online dating services ranging from a variety of demographics. From Christian networks, college students, a mature audience of 50 and up, to online dating for the Deaf, the Jewish, the handicap and disabled – you name it; it's there. According to Match. com, that's 40% of the single people in the U.S. I guess it's safe to say that over the past few years, the methods of dating have changed drastically since its inception.

So what's the hype about this matchmaking biz? According to the Statistic of Brain Research Institute's online data, the total number of single people in the U.S. is estimated to be around 54,250,000, and the total number of people in the U.S. who have tried online dating ranges around 49,250,000 persons. The annual revenue from the online dating industry is continuously on the rise. As they say, they are bringing in Benjamin's baby! Chi Ching! The 21st century has brought about more acceptance and less stigmatization regarding how we seek out relationships, love, and sex. Dating sites have reported many stories of success and happily ever afters. So, with that said, even though the method and perspectives of the world have drastically changed, the message of truth that I present to you today hasn't. Malachi 3:6 reminds us that the Lord does not change. Hebrews 13:8 backs it up reaffirming that Jesus Christ is the same yesterday, today, and forever.

God is love (1 John 4:8). He is the originator, the author, and the creator of love. Nobody can better teach us, show us, or train us how to love than He can.

In these scriptures, God affirms that He is unchanging. Our perspectives, feelings, and emotions change, but God our Creator stays the same and so does His Word. Scripture says it best:

Heaven and earth will pass away, but my words will never pass away. (Matthew 24:35)

CHAPTER 6

The Mountain of Marriage
(God's Perspective on Sex)

God is pro-sex! He created sex as a beautiful expression of love between a man and a woman when it's done within its parameters. In chapter one, we talked about "breaking ground" or consummating.

In the garden, God told Adam and Eve to be fruitful and multiply. It was at that time that He gave His divine approval on sex. God designed the body of a man and the body of a woman to jointly fit together. He made our bodies intrinsically unique and complementary one to the other. God's perspective on sex is not a secret; it can be obtained from many of the Old Testament books as well as the New Testament. God does not want us to be ignorant on any topic; that's why He said in 2 Peter 1:3, His divine power has given us everything we need for a godly life through our knowledge of Him who called us by His own glory and goodness.

Do you desire to know where God stands on certain issues? No need to be perplexed, or bewildered – it's all in His Word.

> For everything that was written in the past was written to teach us, so that through the endurance taught in the scripture and the encouragement they provide we might have hope. (Romans 15:4 NIV)

Today, the hope of rekindling flames and igniting the passion you once had is being offered to you and your spouse.

> Husbands, love your wives, just as Christ loved the church and gave himself up for her. (Ephesians 5:25)

The Word of God likens marriage between a man and woman to Christ and His bride, the church. Are you willing to give up a few things? Are you willing to sacrifice? The scripture just stated that Christ willingly gave Himself up for the church. The same is true in marriage; without sacrifice, there will be no success.

WITHHOLDING – FROM A WOMAN'S PERSPECTIVE

Withholding sexual fulfillment from one another will surely wreak havoc in your marriage. In chapter one, we identified that a man's greatest need is sex. When his spouse does not meet that need, it opens the door for temptation to come knocking in various forms. Through my reading and research for this book, I stumbled upon some data: "Just because a man looks at a woman, it doesn't mean that he's automatically interested in her or is ready to hop into the bed with her." My son once said, "Yeah, Mom, I have to catch myself at times because I have a 'wandering eye.'"

Our previous pastor offered us words of wisdom during premarital counseling session. He said, "Young lady just because you marry him, doesn't mean other women will stop looking. Just like you find him attractive, so will other women. But, guess what young lady; he belongs to you!" He turned to Blake and said, "And young man, the same advice applies to you too!" I know this rings true to many marriages and relationships. We too are guilty. I can't begin to tell you the many times that my husband and I had a confrontation because he "looked." I would ask, "Why are you looking at her?" He would shake his head in dismay and respond, "What did I do?" There on the spot or after seeing him "look" I would just roll my eyes and think to myself, "It's OK [neck roll] mmm, hmm. He ain't getting none tonight!" Can any of you relate to this? What's my advice on how to handle it? First, I believe that when we feel rage and envy, it is because of our own insecurities we are secretly struggling with on the inside. Each of us has something that we are struggling with inwardly.

> *God does not desire for us to be ignorant on any topic.*

Secondly, if your spouse is not giving you that same intense "look," you definitely don't want him giving it to anybody else. As wives, we feel that we should have exclusive rights to those eyes. And lastly, as a married woman, I believe we sometimes feel threatened. What do I mean by that? If your marriage is on the rocks, it's a little shaky. Maybe trust has been broken, and you're experiencing some extreme challenges within your marriage. Then, that act of "looking" puts you in fear as the wife because of your unhealthy marriage. It makes you feel intimidated or that maybe, he's interested in someone else. However, all jealousy is not bad. In the book of Exodus, Moses instructs us that God Himself is a jealous God. But God's jealousy is a holy and just displeasure.

As married women, we need to talk to our spouses and tell them how much it bothers us, pray, and ask God for wisdom and guidance. Perhaps, you're struggling with extreme feelings of jealousy, or maybe he is. Whatever the struggle, God can work through you both to bring peace in your marriage. Continuous outbursts of uncontrolled anger toward your spouse because of the "look" is not healthy for you, beneficial for him or for your marriage – I speak this from experience.

After Blake and I were married, and the babies started coming, I thought to myself, "Dang! Is sex all he wants from me?" I was feeling like, "How many times a week do we have to do it?"

As a newly married wife, this was all very "new" to me. Shoot, I was tired after taking care of my small kids; I didn't feel like having sex every night. That was my mentality at that time. While we were dating, I didn't mind having sex with him all the time. Sex before marriage is totally against the Word of God and His plan for sex and sexual purity. I am just sharing my testimony and life experiences. So again, before Blake and I got married, we tested the waters many times. However, after marriage, we were not making as many waves in the water. Both of us had full-time jobs, and I was attending college, at night. All I wanted was sleep. Often, I was tired and just had no desire, but he did. Those first few years of marriage were very tough. We had to learn, grow, and get to know each other from a whole new perspective, embracing some habits and choices, and tolerating others. Nevertheless, through it all, God's grace was sufficient, and He helped us to put selfishness and pride aside. We've made it to 25 years!

Over the years, we had to learn and grow, consciously choosing to accept God's way of doing things knowing that it is always going to be better and beneficial! We understand that our union was, is, and has been under the grace and protection of God. It is only God's grace and mercy that brought us this far through this "schooling of marriage." By no means do I speak as if we have already graduated or attained perfection, no not in the least. But, I speak this confidently, saying that we are now getting better grades in many of the everyday life marriage courses and choices that we make. And now in my marriage, for me, making waves and going to the mountain top with my husband is better today than when we first met!

WITHHOLDING – FROM A MAN'S PERSPECTIVE

I can remember my wife and I walking into the mall, hand in hand, when a pretty lady walked past us wearing a pair of skin-tight jeans. I slowly turned my head to get a second look, not realizing that my wife was staring at me. "Shoot!!" I mumbled to myself. Instantly, she became furious, dropped my hand, rolled her eyes, and walked off, leaving me behind. Needless to say, it was "quiet time," both verbally and sexually for many days after that. Later, regretting what happened, I thought to myself, "Man, why did I have to look?"

From a man's perspective, we can get used to the quiet time verbally because we understand that women look forward to those one on one conversations and the attention (which are not always the most important things to the man). But the major-ity of women know and understand what keeps a man's interest – sex. Most men like those sweet, intimate, quiet talks and the cuddle time. But, we like that cuddle time, even more, when it ends in sex. At least, that's how I feel.

So, when my wife withheld sex from me, I felt angry. She would be on her side of the bed sleeping while I was laying there upset and furious. I couldn't sleep or figure out why she was acting like I did something wrong. All I did was look! Don't tell me that women don't have any power. Women can often persuade us to do things that our bosses, our friends, our earthly parents, and even our heavenly Father can't convince us to do.

Let's take a trip back to the Garden of Eden. Eve persuaded Adam to eat of the forbidden fruit that God distinctly told him not to eat. Adam had that one on one fellowship with God where he walked daily with Him. But, the woman came along and persuaded her husband to eat of the forbidden fruit, later suffering the consequences of disobedience. God said:

> But of the tree of the knowledge of good and evil, thou shalt not eat of it: for in the day that thou eatest thereof thou shalt surely die. (Genesis 2:17)

We all yield to temptation at times, knowingly or unknowingly. I'm not saying that I didn't know what I was doing when I took the second look. But, as I grow in my relationship with my wife, I try not to repeat those same offenses. I make every effort not to do the things I know will hurt her or give her reason to doubt my commitment, allegiance, and love.

However, women, certain things catch the eyes of a man. Nice cars, sports, and beautiful women are included. So ladies, knowing this, it would be helpful to us if you try to understand and accept the fact that MEN are going to look. That is not to say that your spouse does not find you just as or more attractive than the woman he looked at. And, it does not mean that he is interested in someone else. It's just a man thing! We can't help but appreciate the beauty of the opposite sex. However, once again, men, you have to be smart about the timing of your looks and don't forget to give your wife that same intense kind of look every now and then. Prayerfully, don't allow the look to lead to more.

Lastly, ladies, it's not wise to withhold sex from your spouse for long periods of time. Doing so may influence them to "look" even more. Then, before you know it, "the look" can turn into a search! Real talk!

YOU CAN'T GIVE WHAT YOU DON'T HAVE

God is love, and if we are not connected to the love source, we will not be able to produce or reproduce what we don't have. Whatever I'm trying to create, I must have the proper elements to successfully bring about. For example, if I'm an orange tree, I can't produce or grow apples. I'm an orange tree; I can only reproduce oranges. As we really don't know how to love others the way we should, to sustain a healthy marriage as a Christian, it is essential for that marriage to be centered around Christ. I'm not speaking of only wearing the title "Christian" but to have a relationship with Christ. Our *spiritual* relationship must become a priority. When it is not a priority, we tend to lose our zeal and passion for our first love, Christ.

Have you allowed your marriage to Christ to become dry or unappealing leading you to become spiritually lethargic and apathetic? You hardly ever pray anymore; you barely make it to church on Sundays and your participation to do anything for the Lord has dwindled to little or nothing. You feel, "What's the use," right? For those of you who are Christians and got married in the church but for whatever reason have not been back, this bitter root goes even deeper. And lastly, there are those who feel they don't need God to maintain a successful marriage; they are doing just fine on their own. My husband and I were guilty of this same experience and mindset. Our relationship was thriving; God blessed us with a beautiful wedding, a new home, healthy children, a church family. He was meeting all our needs and more.

However, after the blessings were received, we both made the choice to take a break from church. God knows our hearts, right? So weeks turned into months, and months turned into years. We strayed far away from God, setting our hearts on mammon. Mammon became our god, along with worldly pleasures. Needless to say, after our hearts strayed from God, they also began to stray from each other. I was empty inside, in love with my husband, but not feeling loved by him. Blake had recently bought us our second home – that he refurbished beautifully – *and* a nice car. We were blessed with two beautiful children. I had nice clothes, and at that time, I was working as a stay-at-home mom. Still, I was not happy. My heart longed for love from my husband.

At that time, as a newly married couple, we were both oblivious to the fact that men and women seek love differently. A woman wants to be the top priority in her husband's life. The opportunity to spend quality one on one time with my husband is priceless. I longed for his attention and his time. The clothes were nice; I was thankful for all the material possessions but, I would have given it all up to become his top priority.

Blake was a great provider for our family, we didn't lack anything during the first few years of our marriage, at least from a human perspective, we didn't. But from God's perspective, we were spiritually bankrupt, depleted, miserable, and empty inside. Why? Because God was not first place in our lives. We chose not to give Him a place of priority.

> Seek ye first the Kingdom of God and His righteousness, and all these things shall be added unto you. (Matthew 6:33)

I truly thank God for His mercy and for not treating us as our sins deserve. Our lives were out of order. We didn't realize how far we had fallen until God picked us back up. We were totally ignorant of how far we had drifted into darkness until the light of truth and knowledge began to shine into our situation. We were blind to our dysfunctional marriage. I use the term dysfunctional because our marriage was NOT functioning the way God had intended.

God instituted marriage. He gave us principles to follow so that each and every marriage could have the chance to prosper and flourish the way He designed. Sometimes, we don't know that things aren't working well until they have been fixed. Know this: you need God to have a *successful* marriage, not a *perfect* marriage. The only *perfect* marriage will be the marriage of Christ and His church in glory.

God is able to bless your marriage. He can position it in a place of grace where husbands and wives – through faith, trust, and communication – can overcome daily challenges, fears, disagreements, misunderstandings, problems, and hurts. Marriage is work; I believe I'll say that again! Marriage is work; it is ministry! Just like a garden, it has to be cultivated. A garden has to be attended to for the plants to grow; it needs water, sunlight, pruning, and nourishment. Once the plants begin to grow, sometimes, they will even have to be re-potted.

My personal belief and faith conviction tell me that if you are maintaining a somewhat decent marriage, a marriage outside of God, it truly is by His unfailing love and mercy. But my question to you is why be satisfied with just maintaining a marriage when you can experience a mountaintop marriage? Why not have a marriage that gets better with time as both of you grow and climb together pursuing the wisdom and love of God.

FROM A WOMAN'S PERSPECTIVE – FROM MY HEART TO YOURS

As a wife, it is so important to encourage your spouse. It's vital to respect him, love him, and honor him, just as we promise in our covenant vows. I am learning to become more submissive every day because I value my marriage, and I value my relationship with God. The most hesitant words spoken between couples are "I'm sorry" and "I forgive you." These words carry so much power, yet, we often resist and refuse to humble ourselves to speak them. I know I am guilty. Nevertheless, God has brought me a long way. And, I have much further to go.

I can honestly say that I love my husband more today than I did when I first married him. Our love is climaxing for each other vigorously in many areas more and more each day.

FROM A MAN'S PERSPECTIVE

As a husband, it is extremely important to make your wife feel as though she is the most important thing or person in the world (after God of course). Men, we need to spend time listening to our wives. Those little conversations after you get home from work are very important. I can honestly admit that this is one area that I struggle with though God is helping me to improve. At times, I can become easily distracted by giving the football game, other things, or someone else more attention than my wife. Men, my advice to you is to spend time listening. Instead of always doing things your way, take the time to do the things your wife likes. Watch some of her favorite TV programs, be a listening ear, have romantic dates, text her to say I love you while at work, make simple, considerate gestures. You will be surprised how little sacrifices, go a long way to keeping joy and passion in your marriage.

So, now that we've gotten to the root of the problem – the problem of leaving God out and problem of not including Him in every area of your marriage – we can move forward. First, allow Him to come into our life. It is God's desire for all people to be saved and to come to a knowledge of the truth. Facing the truth about ourselves is not always easy or appealing. Do you need to repent and ask the Lord to forgive you? Have you journeyed down the same path my husband and I did? God wants to heal you spiritually so that the real issues can come to the surface. Only then can He have access to your marriage. Secondly, God is a God of love and forgiveness; He wants us to emulate those same characteristics in our marriages.

I believe you were led to this book at a time that your marriage is on the brink of destruction. I believe that God wants to restore your marriage – do you? Today is the beginning of the process of God healing the man or the woman you fell in love with once upon a time. You can adequately express that love to one another with God being in the midst bestowing His blessings upon your holy union.

Scripture says:

> Whoso findeth a wife findeth a good thing, and obtaineth favour of the LORD. (Proverbs 18:22)

This leads me, ladies, to think that unbelievers or unmarried couples should not be having more enjoyment in the bed than believers. The scripture reveals to us that the favor of God is upon this union. Lovemaking has been ordered and blessed by God. Yes, God Almighty has ordered this event within the bond of marriage. Sex is never described as wrong, dirty or sinful if done within the legal bonds of matrimony. Love making is beautiful between a husband and wife.

INVITING OTHERS INTO YOUR MARRIAGE BED

So, what is God's perspective on inviting others into the marriage bed? Well, scripture informs us in Hebrews 13:4, that the marriage bed must be respected by all, and kept undefiled. In other words, this is a private party between the husband and wife; this is God's way. If you desire more romance, intimacy at a new level or more passionate lovemaking, ask God for the wisdom to make it happen. Be assured of this one thing – no one else is needed between the sheets to fulfill your natural human sexual desire. The only persons required for you to have a mountainous sexual experience are you, your spouse, and God! As you and your spouse become more intimate and draw closer to God, the passionate lovemaking and intimacy you long for will prayerfully become a reality!

Just as any loving parent sets rules, guidelines, and boundaries, God has chosen to do the same as our spiritual Father for our protection. The Word of God instructs us to preserve sex for marriage. Our God is infinite and wise. He knows the emotional entanglement, the stresses of pre-marital sex, the devastation of adultery, the danger of diseases, and even the risk of unwanted pregnancies. After the husband and wife have committed to each other in holy matrimony, sex is blessed. The marital union is a depiction of the love of Christ and His church; God desires to be included.

We've all heard the expression that everything that glitters is not gold and everything that looks good is not necessarily good for you. Would you agree with me that love is a very powerful and strong emotion? Would you also agree that one person's perception of love may differ from another based on their past experiences and upbringing? Love impacts our choices; love can influence us to act totally out of our character; love can bring out the best in us or the worst in us and love has the power to persuade or convince us to do things we would never have imagined.

Any unresolved issues can result in a woman withholding sex from her husband. That's why it's so critical for both partners to talk about problems, apologize, forgive, and strive for improvement with God's help. Let's be honest ladies: there is a lot of temptation out there and withholding sexual fulfillment from our spouses is not a wise choice. We already covered the important needs of a man and the important needs of a woman. After marriage, a man expects to have his sexual needs fulfilled by his wife. If his wife neglects to do so, it will create a void and emptiness that he longs to be filled. It can also open a spiritual door for Satan to tempt him with suggestions of how he could be satisfied elsewhere – the same goes for women. My body no longer belongs to me but to my spouse:

> The wife does not have authority over her own body but yields it to her husband. In the same way, the husband does not have authority over his own body but yields it to his wife. (1 Corinthians 7:4 NIV)

> In your anger do not sin: do not let the sun go down while you are still angry. (Ephesians 4:26 NIV)

On the flip side, if sickness has invaded your body, and you're not physically able to have sex, God's grace and power are sufficient to cover your marriage and to sustain it throughout time.

However, that is an entirely different circumstance but with God nothing is impossible.

Whatever the crisis, hope is being offered to those who are struggling within their marriage. Today, hope is being presented and proposed to you before you call it quits. Give me a few more minutes of your time and keep reading this book. You feel so frustrated; you may feel like you don't know what to do. But before you call a divorce attorney, please, keep reading. Before you let go and walk out on everything and everyone, please, read on. (I pray God's presence over you right now, in Jesus' name). Don't throw your hands up just yet. Before you say, "I'm fed up, and I can't take any more"… before you entertain those demonic thoughts of committing suicide… before you retaliate and then later regret it… before you take those pills… before you continue that affair or start a new affair… before you decide to end it all… please wait! You are important; you are loved; you have worth! I can see just a little bit more fight in you. I believe your marriage still has a chance; if it didn't, God wouldn't have sent you this book! Would you kneel and pray with me, please?

Prayer of Restoration

Heavenly Father, in Jesus' name, I believe that Jesus is the Son of God. I believe that He died on the cross and rose on the third day with all power. Please forgive me of my sins. Jesus, I receive You as *my* Lord and Savior. Thank You for Your grace and mercy. Lord, I come to You on behalf of my marriage. My marriage is in shambles. I'm not sure what happened or where it all began, but Dear Lord, please have mercy on me and my spouse during this difficult time. Lord, I choose to put my trust and faith in You to restore our union. I confess: for years, I've tried to do things my way and they didn't work out. We are both guilty of making plans, yet never including You. Lord, I'm calling on You to help us in our time of need. *Right now* I surrender to You! In Jesus' name, I pray for godly wisdom as You begin to rebuild our marriage. Lord, I feel like I am ready to give up on everything. Help me Jesus! Restore unto me the joy of Your salvation. I have so much anger and resentment from my past and for the people that have caused me so much pain. Even in my marriage, there has been so much pain. Lord, please help me to heal inwardly. I admit that I have carried a lot of anger and frustration from my past into my present. In return, this caused some of the problems in my marriage. Lord, help me make it through this difficult time of loneness, pain, frustration, resentment and hurt. Lord, I relinquish my ways for Yours. I deeply desire a closer walk with You. Father, You said that if I draw nigh unto You, You draw nigh unto me. Lord, pour Your presence out over me right now, in the name of Jesus. Lord, be glorified! Teach me how to serve You so that I can know how to serve my spouse and others. Grace me with a tender heart of forgiveness because You have forgiven me for so much! Guide me by Your Holy Spirit in the way of wisdom and truth and let it fortify me. I thank You for restoring me. I thank You for rebuilding my marriage. I thank You for healing me and my spouse emotionally, mentally and spiritually. I accept that it will be a process but Your Word says, in Romans 8:31, if God is for us, who can be against us? In Jesus' name I pray. Amen.

CHAPTER 7

Let's Heal Together

Healing! What is healing? Why do we need healing? And who needs healing? First of all, healing is bringing something that is broken or abnormal into a state of repair or restoration. At times during your marriage, there will be some kind of brokenness or despair that will require healing. Isaiah said:

> He was wounded for our transgressions bruised for our iniquities, the chastisement of our peace was upon him, and by his stripes we are healed. (Isaiah 53:5)

This was a prophecy of the coming suffering servant (Jesus Christ). Jesus was coming to a diseased sin-sick world to provide healing for our sin-sick souls and to heal our relationships with God and one another. Healing is also vital in our marriages. It is a guarantee that you or your spouse are going to do something stupid along the way. You're going to ignore your wife while she's talking to you, you might forget an important day, you might come home late because you were hanging out with the "boys." I can remember a time when my wife's best friend and husband, Kenny, came over for dinner. We were having a great evening until we needed something from the store. To this day, I don't remember exactly what it was, but I can tell you it turned into a long night.

Kenny and I went to the store, a couple of bars and only God knows where else. We left our wives and our children at my house, and we were gone all night. My wife and her friend started to worry about us as the hours rolled on – 10 o'clock, 11 o'clock, midnight, 2 AM. They started to get nervous, thinking something bad had happened. My wife, her friend, and our children got into the car and started looking for us. They drove around practically all night. Finally, they found us early the next morning. I was sleeping in the car half drunk, and Kenny was in the bar.

I know you might not have done anything as stupid as Kenny and I did. To this day, we still laugh and wonder why we did something so dumb. My wife was very upset, but to my surprise, she was more thankful that I was OK. My point is, we are all going to do something for which we will have to ask for forgiveness and bring healing to some situation in our marriage.

I speak confidently on the subject of healing and forgiveness as it relates to my own personal experiences and mistakes, after being married for twenty five years. So, my friend, keep this in mind and remember that you are going to experience some situations where it gets a little quiet in your home. There will be times when you don't agree and times when you don't like your spouse. Note, I said don't like, I didn't say, you don't love because you are to always love your spouse even when he or she makes you angry.

Just recently, I preached a sermon entitled "You're Not Alone" from the following verse:

> Be strong and of a good courage, fear not, nor be afraid of them: for the Lord thy God, he it is that doth go with thee; he will not fail thee, nor forsake thee. (Deuteronomy 31:6)

In the scripture, Moses was encouraging the children of Israel not to feel they were alone. In this life and in your marriage, you're going to feel as though you have been abandoned. Sometimes, we can make our spouses feel like we have abandoned them. This happens when things get out of order; I know this by experience, and I'm still working on it.

God is a God of order. He expects that we will be orderly. Our lives should be structured so that God is FIRST and foremost, then our spouses, our families and after that everything else. Maybe, you get it wrong sometimes. Maybe you put your job or career first, or you put family (parents or children) first and leave your spouse feeling all alone. This encourages infidelity. It creates an opportunity for your spouse to have an affair. Please, my friend, make sure that you examine the order of priorities in your life. I have learned, and I am still learning, that my wife takes precedence over everyone and everything, except God.

> *Always love your spouse, even when they make you angry.*

Thank God for healing. My wife is a God-fearing and loving woman. I'm not saying everything is perfect because we all have flaws. However, God is working on them through the sanctification process of our salvation. But, my wife has always been my biggest encourager. I have seen many marriages fail because of nagging and lack of encouragement. When my wife and I got married back in 1992, I bought a house fixed it up and my wife, my son, and I lived there. My dad, who is now deceased, was amazed at the price that I paid for the house and how nice it turned out. He was a very successful entrepreneur, started buying abandoned houses, which he and I renovated as rental homes. During the process, my dad helped me by financing my first house. I was able to sell it for a profit and buy other homes as rental properties. With the help of God and my dad, I was able to provide a good living for my wife and children through my rental properties. It even came to the point at which my wife and I were able to build a new home. It was the most beautiful home that I have ever seen. But as time went on, our hometown begin to experience financial difficulties. This had a domino effect.

Tenants weren't able to pay their rent and vacant houses were vandalized and stripped of any value they had. It was difficult to insure houses, which caused a lot of people including me to walk away from a lot of properties. My wife and I started to struggle financially, and I was very depressed. God and the encouragement of my wife brought me through. As mentioned earlier, my wife and I built a new home, but because of all the financial difficulties, we faced foreclosure. This brought me to a low point in my life, and God knew that I needed healing.

I was searching for a job because rental income went from great to not even paying the bills. I had to find work. This was very hard to do in a city that was economically challenged. The only thing that kept me going during these difficult times was my wife's encouragement. She would tell me, "Baby you can do it!" "I know God is going to bless you with a job to support our family." There wasn't one time that she nagged or complained. So, ladies, I want you to know that it means everything to show your husbands that you are there to encourage and lift them up. Thank God for my wife!

CHAPTER 8
They Did What?

Learn from the successes and mistakes of others in the Bible. God revealed His original plans for marriage through Adam and Eve's holy union. He divinely instituted it as a sacred ordinance between man and woman. Then, He bestowed blessings upon them both.

Satan's mission is to destroy marriages. He took the opportunity to twist the truth in the Garden of Eden when he lied to Eve. As a result, Eve and her husband Adam were led away from the will of God, causing sin and the consequences of sin to enter their lives. Realistically speaking, we know that resisting Satan, temptation, and our flesh is not always easy. However, with the grace and help of God, we can seek forgiveness, overcome our mistakes, and continue our marriage building process. We can keep striving for healthy, strong, marriages and maintaining a solid foundation in Christ.

*Be careful of the naysayers and the marriage haters speaking things contrary to God's Word about your spouse or your marriage!

Build and "Wait" Patiently!

Abraham and Sarah received a promise from God, a promise that would not be fulfilled until the appointed time. Wait for your appointed time; it's coming!

Unwanted Bricks

Interfering with the plans of God due to impatience and leaning to your own understanding.

Build on Endurance

Jacob's love for Rachel helped him to endure many pains related to his relationship. Jacob deeply loved and cherished Rachel. He willingly and patiently worked for his bride and did whatever was in his power to make her happy. Building a marriage requires staying until the job is done.

Unwanted Bricks

Competing with others, discontentment, allowing things to validate our worth, seeking things from our spouses that only God can give, deceiving one another, and lying.

Build on Trust

God did something extraordinary through an ordinary couple. Joseph's and Mary's lives can be classic examples to many of us; they brought glory to God through their obedience. God, our Father, chose these two ordinary people to become the earthly parents of our Lord and Savior, Jesus Christ. What an awesome privilege! Has God chosen to do something extraordinary through you and your spouse or your marriage? Are you willing to respond as Mary did? "I am the Lord's servant; May Your word to me be fulfilled

> "I am the Lord's servant," Mary answered. "May your word to me be fulfilled." Then the angel left her. (Luke 1:38 NIV)

Mary was favored by God; she and Joseph were divinely chosen. However, that did not exempt them from life's problems and dilemmas. They had to face bitterness before they possessed their blessing!

God is able to make beautiful what was once ugly in our marriages. The bitterness you are now facing could one day become your greatest blessing – a blessing that in turn will help to build, shape, and save other marriages, not just your own.

Unwanted Bricks

Only thinking of self and an unwillingness to follow God!

> *The wisdom of God should always prevail over human indifferences.*

Build on Prayer

In Elkanah and Hannah's marriage, Hannah used prayer to take her through her season of barrenness. In her time of shame, frustration, brokenness, and grief, Hannah put herself at the mercy of God. Humbly kneeling at the altar in the temple, she cried out to her Creator during one of the most challenging times in her life. Hannah desperately desired a child, and she knew that only God could satisfy her most innate desire.

What area in your marriage do you feel is barren, unproductive, or bleak? Are you willing to go to God in prayer as Hannah did? Are you willing to surrender your situation to God and trust Him for the results? God sees your pain, just like He saw Hannah's. Are you ready to cry out to God on behalf of your marriage? Only He can help you pick up the broken pieces and guide you through your rebuilding process. Will you trust Him to give you beauty for your ashes? Hannah did! And lastly, do you have faith that He is able to birth life back into your "lifeless" marriage? Keep P.U.S.H.I.N.G... **P**ray **U**ntil **S**omething **H**appens It's **I**n **G**od's Hands!"

He is able to impregnate your marriage with joy, vibrancy, love, excitement, and passion!

Unwanted Bricks

Revenge, self-pity, giving up.

Build on the Wisdom of God

Marriages hold three perspectives as we discussed earlier. Often, when differences arise, most people think that their ways, opinions or solutions are best. However, when there is a conflict of opinion between you and your wife, the wisdom of God should always prevail. When spouses collaboratively agree that God's way is right, they gain an automatic victory for their marriage. I once heard from my wise pastor, "Let us agree that we disagree." When we cannot agree and find common ground with one another, we should indeed be able to agree with what the Word of God says. Disputes and differences should easily be settled when we seek the wisdom of God and apply His principles to the problem – even if it's not easy, it will be profitable.

David praised Abigail for her good judgment.

> David said to Abigail, "Praise be to the LORD, the God of Israel, who has sent you today to meet me. May you be blessed for your good judgment and for keeping me from bloodshed this day and from avenging myself with my own hands. (1 Samuel 25:32-33)

Abigail was a woman who strived to make the best out of a very difficult situation. The Bible describes her as beautiful, generous, and intelligent, but her husband Nabal was evil and harsh. In marriages where the spouses seem to be total opposites, seeking godly wisdom through prayer is crucial for their well-being. The constant friction of your opinions, choices, ideas, perspectives, suggestions, and marriage in general can only be solaced by God and godly wisdom.

Unwanted Bricks

Arrogance, greed, selfishness, and folly.

Build on Unconditional Love

> And now these three remain: faith, hope and love. But the greatest of these is love. (1 Corinthians 13:13 NIV)

Hosea, an Old Testament prophet, and his wife Gomer are pictures of God's love and faithfulness to His often unloving and unfaithful people Israel. God commanded faithful Hosea to marry a woman who in return would be unfaithful. She was a woman who would be guilty of causing him many heartaches. The book of Hosea is a love story – a real true love story – that dramatically portrays our God's constant and persistent love toward His adulterous people Israel. For Hosea, the struggle of being married to an unfaithful woman was real. Equally so, however, was the forgiveness that he extended to her after she committed many wrongs within their marriage.

We serve an awesome God, a God who continuously forgives, loves, and remains faithful to us even when we are not faithful to Him. Just like Gomer.

As married couples, it is vital to build our marriages on unconditional love. Unconditional love is not moved or swayed by emotions or feelings. Loving someone unconditionally requires sacrifice. Unconditional love is not based on conditions – "If you do this, then, I will do that." No! Unconditional love says, whether you do your part or not, I am committed to doing mine! This is the kind of love that God has for us; with the help of God, it is attainable. What makes me so confident to say that? My own marriage!

God's love for us is solid and with His help, the love you have for your spouse can be just as strong and unconditional.

CHAPTER 9

It's a Covenant

What is a covenant? A covenant is an agreement between God and man or His people to do or not do something specified. A covenant, in its most general and historical sense, is a solemn promise to engage in or refrain from a specified action. Here are some examples of covenants.

The Edenic Covenant (Genesis 1:28) – God made a covenant with Adam and Eve in the Garden of Eden before sin entered. God conveyed His purpose for creation.

The Adamic Covenant (Genesis 3:14) – This covenant was also given to Adam and Eve in the Garden before they were cast from it.

The Noahic Covenant (Genesis 9:1) – This covenant was between God and Noah. After the flood, God promised that He would never again destroy all life on Earth with a flood. God gave the rainbow as the sign of the covenant, a promise that He would never flood the entire earth again with water.

The Abrahamic Covenant (Genesis 15:18) – In this covenant, God promised many things to Abraham.

The Mosaic Covenant (Exodus 19:25) – The Mosaic Covenant was a conditional covenant that either brought God's blessings for obedience or God's curses for disobedience upon the nation of Israel.

The Davidic Covenant (2 Samuel 7:16) – God promised that David's lineage would last forever.

The Palestinian Covenant (Deuteronomy 30:1-10) – This covenant is given to Israel and is conditioned upon their repentance.

The New Covenant (Hebrews 8:8) – Rests upon the sacrifices of Christ. Under The New Covenant, all are now given the opportunity to receive salvation as a free gift.

> For by grace are ye saved through faith; and that not of yourselves: it is the gift of God: Not of works, lest any man should boast. (Ephesians 2:8-9)

As you can see, God has established covenants with men since the beginning of time, including marriage covenants. God has communicated His will and plans to His people by establishing covenants. As we read earlier, God made vows to do things for His covenanted people, some of which were conditional and some of which were unconditional. In biblical times, covenants were binding, they were important, and they were very serious, just like marriages.

A marriage covenant is a sacred bond between a man and a woman instituted by and publicly entered into before God. Marriage is not a contract.

A contract is an agreement between two or more persons signifying that all signing parties will do something. Penalties may be included if the contract is breached (if they don't do what was agreed upon). Contracts are not based on trust, but a covenant is based on trust. Also, contracts are only for a limited time and typically have an expiration date. On the other hand, covenants are initiated by God; they do not expire.

In Genesis, we are given the account of how God presented Adam's bride to him.

So the Lord God caused a deep sleep to come over the man, and he slept. God took one of his ribs and closed the flesh at that place. Then the Lord God created a woman from the rib He had taken from the man and brought her to the man. And the man said: "This one, at last, is bone of my bone and flesh of my flesh; this one will be called 'woman,' for she was taken from man. (Genesis 2:21-23 NIV)

The very first marriage is recorded in the Holy Bible, in the Garden of Eden, with God as the Holy Officiator of this auspicious wedding. Can you visualize it? Yes, right there in the beautiful garden, with Adam as the groomsman and Eve as his bride. I'm confident that this was one of the most beautiful and breathtaking day of eternity. It was all God's doing and as Scripture informs us, He does all things well!

> *Marriage is a covenant between a man and a woman, not a contract.*

Can you picture our heavenly Father escorting Eve? At the voice of His command navigating her to her groom, guiding her every footstep (be it many or few) as He presents her to her husband, her spouse of covenant. God, our heavenly Father, is all-knowing; He knew before the beginning of time that these two were truly a match to be made in Heaven. Everything was divinely coordinated as God graciously joined the two of them together as man and wife by the power vested in Him! Adam then said, "This is now bone of my bones, and flesh of my flesh, she shall be called 'woman' for she was taken out of man."

I can only imagine Adam and Eve's wedding day being superior to all those that would come after. On this day, it was God, Himself, setting the standards and principles for all marriages. I am confident that it was the wedding of all weddings – a wedding that our majestic and holy God put His divine stamp of approval on. It was certainly a holy union that originated from and was instituted and intrinsically designed by God. This union was in His very own sanctuary, which was adorned and filled with all His glory and splendor, radiating ever so brightly because, well, He is God!

The book of Ecclesiastes tells us there is a season and a time for everything. It was this exact moment in time that God chose to unite these two people. It was through this union that our great God made a visible picture of His deep unconditional love for mankind. He also used this union to symbolically show the love that He would one day lavish on His covenanted people, Israel. It was symbolic of Christ and His love for His beloved bride – the church.

CHAPTER 10

The Bride of Christ

According to Dr. Robert Clouse and Steve Gregg, when reading the book of Revelation, you need to understand that there are different views of and approaches to written prophecy. In the opening verses of Revelation 19, the wedding day for Christ and His Church is proclaimed.

> Let us rejoice and be glad and give him glory! For the wedding of the Lamb has come, and his bride has made herself ready. Fine linen, bright and clean, was given her to wear. (Fine linen stands for the righteous acts of God's holy people.) Then the angel said to me, "Write this: Blessed are those who are invited to the wedding supper of the Lamb!" And he added, "These are the true words of God." At this I fell at his feet to worship him. But he said to me, "Don't do that! I am a fellow servant with you and with your brothers and sisters who hold to the testimony of Jesus. Worship God! For it is the Spirit of prophecy who bears testimony to Jesus." (Revelation 19:7-10 NIV)

To better understand this prophecy, we need to understand the perspective of the writer and the Jewish culture of that time. William Hendriksen, Finis Jennings Dake, and many other Bible scholars explain that the Jewish marriage customs at that time, from which the biblical imagery is derived, began with the betrothal of the bride and groom, which was as binding as marriage itself. At that time, the period of the engagement allowed the groom to pay the dowry to the father of the bride. It also gave the bride the opportunity to prepare for the wedding just as God is allowing us time to prepare for the second coming of Christ.

In this controversial scripture, the question, "Who exactly is the bride of Christ?" has been pondered from many different angles.

William MacDonald responds to this question and states his views in the ever so popular *Believer's Bible Commentary.* He writes, "The church is the heavenly Bride." However, there are many who oppose this particular view and some who side with this view only in part.

Paul writes to the church at Corinth:

> I am jealous for you with a godly jealousy. I promised you to one husband, to Christ, so that I might present you as a pure virgin to him. (2 Corinthians 11:2 NIV)

To better understand this scripture as well as many others, it's vital to keep this in mind:

> Do your best to present yourself to God as one approved, a worker who does not need to be ashamed and who correctly handles the word of truth. (2 Timothy 2:15 NIV)

So with that, we conclude by saying, pray for God's truth to be revealed to you and then act on it.

THE BRIDEGROOM AND THE BRIDE

Submit to one another out of reverence for Christ:

> Wives, submit yourselves to your own husbands as you do to the Lord. For the husband is the head of the wife as Christ is the head of the church, his body, of which he is the Savior. Now as the church submits to Christ, so also wives should

submit to their husbands in everything. Husbands, love your wives, just as Christ loved the church and gave himself up for her to make her holy, cleansing her by the washing with water through the word, and to present her to himself as a radiant church, without stain or wrinkle or any other blemish, but holy and blameless. In this same way, husbands ought to love their wives as their own bodies. He who loves his wife loves himself. After all, no one ever hated their own body, but they feed and care for their body, just as Christ does the church for we are members of his body. "For this reason a man will leave his father and mother and be united to his wife, and the two will become one flesh." This is a profound mystery—but I am talking about Christ and the church. However, each one of you also must love his wife as he loves himself, and the wife must respect her husband. (Ephesians 5:21-33 NIV)

> *Pray for God's truth to be revealed to you, and then act on it.*

In the apostle Paul's letter to the church of Ephesus, he uses the illustration of a marriage relationship to teach the relationship of Christ to His church. The word "church" is the English translation of the Greek word *ekklesia*, which means "assembly" or a congregation of "called out ones." Eve was divinely made and chosen for Adam; the same is true pertaining to the church (the called out body) of believers; they too have been divinely chosen for Christ as His bride.

The LORD God caused a deep sleep to fall upon Adam, and he slept; then God took one of Adam's ribs and closed up the flesh at that place. The LORD God fashioned into a woman the rib which He had taken from the man, and brought her to the man, Adam then said, 'This is now bone of my bones, and flesh of my flesh; She shall be called Woman, Because she was taken out of Man.' (Genesis 2:21-23)

The Lord made Adam's beautiful bride, Eve, by taking a rib from his side! Similarly, our last Adam's bride was taken from His side. According to 1 Corinthians 15:45, Jesus, our last Adam, was horrifically beaten; He suffered, bled and died for the sins of many (Hebrews 9:28).

When he had received the drink, Jesus said, 'It is finished.' With that, he bowed his head and gave up his spirit. (John 19:30)

After uttering the words, "It is finished," Jesus fell into the "sleep of death." According to Clarence Larkins, this "sleep of death" would cause the church to be formed after Jesus was thrust in His side with a spear (John 19:34).

The Bible records that our first Adam's bride was taken from his side, and according to many accredited theologians and our own personal studies, the same holds true of our last Adam, Christ. From his side, His bride, the church was formed.

If you desire to be a part of the greatest, grandest wedding of all time, an invitation is being extended for you. On that day, we will stand in the very presence of God as "the bride of Christ," collectively with all the other saints, awaiting marriage to the Holy Lamb of God.

Jesus has already made a way for each and every person to be included in this special day, but the decision is yours. There is no need to worry about your wedding garments or the ceremonial arrangements because our Lord and Savior Jesus Christ has already taken care of everything for you at His own expense.

If you declare with your mouth, "Jesus is Lord," and believe in your heart that God raised him from the dead, you will be saved. For it is with your heart that you believe and are justified, and it is with your mouth that you profess your faith and are saved. (Romans 10:9-10 NIV)

Accept Jesus as your Lord and Savior today, repeat after me:

I believe and confess that Jesus Christ is the Son of God and that He died on the cross for my sins. His death, burial, and resurrection were for me. I now receive Jesus as my personal Lord and Savior. I thank You, heavenly Father, for forgiving me of all my sins. I thank You, heavenly Father, for Your grace and mercy. In Jesus' name, I pray. Amen!

Welcome to God's family. Find a church home where you can begin to grow more in the knowledge and grace of Jesus.

Revelation 19:7 says, "the bride of the Lamb" was given fine linen to wear, bright and pure. Oh, what a glorious honor and privilege we have been given as the children of God. One day, we will be wedded in holy matrimony to Jesus Christ, the Holy Lamb of God! Jesus loves you! Continue to prepare for His second coming by praying, studying, and reading about the bridegroom. We thank God for you, and we look forward to seeing you at the marriage supper of the Lamb!

TWENTY-DAY
Marriage Devotional

It is our prayer that each and every time you read these devotionals and pray, the anointing of the Holy Spirit will consume you with His presence.

> You fill me with joy in your presence, with eternal pleasures at your right hand. (Psalm 16:11 NIV)

So, as you read and pray these anointed devotions, expect results. If it's a healing devotion, expect healing; if it's a deliverance devotion, expect deliverance; if it's a chain breaking request, then expect chains to be broken over your marriage. Allow the Holy Spirit to have free reign in your union as He knocks down some walls, and rebuild others. Allow the Holy Spirit to rule and reign as He directs your steps and gives you the wisdom to rekindle flames and spark passion in your marriage. Please, don't give up yet. Keep fighting, keep praying, keep fasting and keep praising. The best is yet to come.

For twenty days, purpose in your heart to seek God with your spouse or individually. If you need to incorporate fasting, then fast as you seek God. Relinquish your ways for His. God is able to help – if you let Him.

Keep in mind, it may not happen overnight; Sarah and Abraham waited more than twenty years for the promise of God to be fulfilled. Solomon reminds us in the book of Ecclesiastes that better is the end of a thing than the beginning. Marriage is a ministry, and ministry is work. Today, you can make the choice to start re-building your marriage from the ground up. Many tools have already been provided to you in this book. Now, it is time to put them to use! You are not alone, and you are not without hope.

Sincerely,
Rev. & Mrs. Scott

DAY 1

He Is Listening

He will call on me, and I will answer him; I will be with him in trouble, I will deliver him and honor him. (Psalm 91:15)

I yelled from another room, "Blake!" "Blake!!" "Blake!!!" Still, no response. I thought to myself: "Now, I *know* he heard me," while at the same time wondering, "Why is he not answering me?" Aggravated, I got up from my computer and walked toward our family room to see what was happening. I heard deep snoring vibrating from the walls. As I got closer and closer, I began shaking my head as I glanced over at the sofa to look at Blake. I let out a soft chuckle, thinking to myself "Wow! He is fast asleep." Still shaking my head, I turned around to go back into my office, happy he wasn't ignoring me after all. I started to tiptoe softly out of the family room so that I would not wake him. But, before I could even take a few steps, Blake gently lifted his head and said, "Hey babe! Whatcha doing?"

I turned around and replied, "Oh, nothing. I was just checking on you. I was calling you for the longest time, and you didn't respond, so I just came to see what was up. I wanted to show you something on the computer."

"Oh, I'm sorry, babe," said Blake. "I was *knocked out* sleeping."

How many times have you called out for someone to get his or her attention, maybe your spouse, a child, a co-worker or friend? You called out their names, over and over again, yet, you got no response. You may have even become irritated thinking that they were intentionally ignoring you.

Well today, as children of God, we can certainly give thanks and praise to Him for His Word. Scripture assures us that God never slumbers or sleeps, and He does not become weary. Isn't that good news? I mean with caller ID, cell phones, texting, face time – let's face it, sometimes, people are just not available. They are busy, or tired. Maybe they *are* guilty of ignoring us. Whatever the reason, we can be strengthened as we cling to the truth of knowing that God promises to answer us. His love and mercies never end; they are new every morning.

Psalms 91:15 speaks to our hearts that God hears us; He is with us, He will deliver us, and He brings honor to us as His children for honoring Him. Maybe, you have been calling out to God on behalf of your marriage. Just like I didn't get a response from Blake, you feel that you haven't gotten a response from God. Be encouraged, keep calling on Him. Keep crying out to God through prayer. Keep calling His name on behalf of your marriage and your children. God's promises are true; He is faithful to do what He said He will do. So, until He answers you, keep calling Him! And then listen. Keep your ears and eyes open for His response, which will more than likely come through His Word, your minister, a friend, and perhaps, even, in a still small voice. Until then dear one, know with assurance that God is with you as you go through the storm!

Prayer

Thank You, Lord, for Your promise to answer us, to be with us, to deliver us and to honor us. Lord, we call out to You right now on behalf of our marriages. In Jesus' name, I ask You to deliver us from anything that's hindering our relationship with You. Awaken us out of our spiritual sleep and help us to draw closer to You. Protect us and protect our children. Lord, help our marriage to be a reflection of Your unconditional love and forgiveness so that others can be helped, healed and that You will be glorified in our union. In Jesus' precious name, I pray. Amen!

DAY 2

Turn Up the Heat

And she said to them, 'Call me not Naomi, call me Mara:
for the Almighty has dealt very bitterly with me.' (Ruth 1:20)

"Brrr! It is freezing out here" (shivering as I walk to my car). "I should have added more layers; this winter weather is no joke." *"Brrrr!"* (as the snow and the temperature continue to fall). Finally, after a brisk walk, I arrived at my car. I hurriedly got in and immediately adjusted the thermostat, increasing it to the max. "Oh wow, it is a bitterly cold day!"

Yes, seasons do change and let me be the first to tell you that winter is not my favorite season. The snow is beautiful, but the cold weather that accompanies it can be unpleasant. Sometimes, the frigid temperatures require that you put on layers of clothing and to really dress the part!

Has the temperature changed in your marriage? What about in the bedroom? Does it feel cold and drafty in there with your spouse? Maybe, you're feeling like the romance temperature has drastically dropped and the fire has gone out. It seems that your affection for one another has become frigid and cold. You both have layered yourselves with anger, resentment, unforgiveness, and pain. The layers are so thick that neither of you knows where to begin or which piece to take off first.

I am reminded of a story in the book of Ruth. Naomi, Ruth's mother-in-law, said, "Don't call me Naomi, call me Mara, because the Almighty has made my life very bitter" (Ruth 1:20). Naomi, whose name initially meant pleasant, became very bitter because she had lost so much. She felt that the pleasures and joys of life had ended after her loved ones passed away. Naomi said, "bitterness and sadness are now my lot."

Maybe, circumstances have caused you to become bitter in your marriage, just like Naomi. The bitterness has robbed you of your drive to make love to your spouse, to be affectionate and just show you care. Maybe, you have even lost your will to fight for your marriage. In a sense, Naomi was the same way. At one time in her life, everything was so pleasant – that's what her name meant. Then, the seasons changed in her life and maybe, in yours too.

As a child, I was always taught that wearing a swim suit at the beach is perfectly fine in the summer months, but if it's snowing outside, and I put on swimming attire, I could possibly catch a cold or get sick. Well, let's apply that same principle to marriages. For example, when we refuse to put on the correct clothing that Christ has provided for us as Christians, we are prone to catch a cold. In other words, we may catch cold feelings towards each other. Increasingly, we will become more and more bitter with more layers (problems) being added daily, one by one. Like colds, there are no quick fixes, they just have to run their course. Sometimes, different medicines can speed up the healing and provide relief while you wait for the cold to fully go away.

Will you allow God to help you take off those layers? According to the Bible, wearing too much clothing can easily weigh you down:

> Therefore, since we are surrounded by such a great cloud of witnesses, let us throw off everything that hinders and the sin that so easily entangles. And let us run with perseverance the race marked out for us. (Hebrews 12:1 NIV)

Are you willing to let God rekindle that fire between you and your spouse? Are you willing to let Him get the flames burning in the bedroom, once again? Today, if this is your desire, you can decide to let God provide you with the medicine (His Word) that will give you temporary relief while you wait for complete deliverance and for the "cold" season to pass.

Will you pray this prayer and commit to a three-day fast, believing God to break off some of your chains? Are you willing to stand for your marriage as Christ stood for the church? You're not alone. God is with you, and He loves you.

Prayer

Heavenly Father, we come to You in Jesus' name. Holy Spirit, You are welcome into my heart. Holy Spirit, You are welcome into my marriage. Please, forgive me of my sins in Jesus' name. I confess that I have weighed myself down with sin; the layers are so thick, Lord, I don't even know where to begin or how to take them off. Jesus, I surrender myself and my marriage to You. Rekindle, restore, renew, rebuild, and revive my marriage. Lord. I'm not seeking a perfect marriage, but I am seeking a perfect God who has a perfect will, and a God who specializes in the impossible. Today, Lord, I commit the impossible to You. I humbly ask that You soften both of our hearts, help us to forgive each other and heal our union. In Jesus' name, I pray. Amen.

DAY 3

First Not Last

But seek first his kingdom and his righteousness, and all these things will be given to you as well. (Matthew 6:33)

Recently, I woke up thinking about my beautiful little ten-year-old niece Javana. A few weeks ago, Javana played her first basketball game, and boy was she excited. She had set her alarm clock the night before to make sure that she woke up on time for the game. While still in bed, I heard Javana in the bathroom running water brushing her teeth. Afterward, I saw her go into her room to get dressed. After around thirty minutes or so, Javana came out looking gamed up in her sports attire. She called, "Aunt Lisa, I'm ready!"

"OK, baby!" I yelled out to her. "Let me get my coat on." So we both got into the car and prepared to leave. After a short drive to the opposing team's school, we pulled up in the parking lot. Before I could turn off the ignition, Javana hopped out of the car and briskly walked to the door of the school. After entering the school, she went directly to the gym looking for her teammates and her coach. All the girls were super excited.

The coach finally arrived, and the girls on her team all went into the bathroom to change into their uniforms. They regathered in the gym fully changed. After a few warm-up drills, the whistle blew and the coaches and referees beckoned each team to the middle of the basketball court. It was time for the game to begin!

The first quarter was a bit hilarious, to say the least, the score was 0 - 0. To our surprise, the second quarter changed somewhat; the girls on Javana's team were fierce, and they really stepped up their game. "What!" as I looked out on the floor, it was Javana dribbling the ball, swerving in and out between her opponents, making her way down the court. Then, she tilted her hands, threw the ball in the air and made her very first basket – *Swoosh!!!* The crowd went crazy, "YEAHHH!!!" Everyone was filled with excitement. Javana's teammate made a basket and then there was another one from a different player.

In the third quarter and Javana's team was leading. However, in the fourth quarter, everything drastically changed; the opposing team scored multiple points, taking the lead and ultimately winning the game. After the game, Javana and her teammates came over crying and discouraged. They lamented that the other girls were not being fair: "They were hitting and pushing us. I can't believe we came in last! I don't like last place!" said Javana.

In a marriage, that can often be the number one complaint from either spouse: "I don't like the last place" and rightfully so. On your wedding day, you stood at the altar and made a solemn oath before God and family to "forsake all others." That sacred covenant meant that your spouse would take first place in your life, a place of precedence, after God. I know life happens, and we all tend to get busy with our children, families, ministries, church, work, hobbies, friends, me time and so forth. Sometimes, we allow our list of priorities to be misconstrued by distractions from "all these things" quoted directly from the Bible. And "these things" slowly begin to push our spouses and families out of first place. The same applies to God.

The Bible says to seek God first:

Seek first God's kingdom and what God wants. Then all your other needs will be met as well. (Matthew 6:33 NCV)

Believe it or not, God does not like the last place either. He says, "I am a jealous God." So most likely, if God is not first in your marriage then your entire list of priorities will be out of order.

So, what can we do to make things right? Well, just like basketball, there are rules to the game. The outline has been given in Scripture. Today, you can begin renewing your relationship with God, giving Him His rightful place as your personal coach. Take time to pray, read His Word, and to just thank Him. You will begin to learn more about Him. At the same time, He will begin to show you more about yourself and your marriage. You may even need to attend a Christian bible study (Hebrews 10:25) where you can receive help to better prepare for the "game of marriage." There are many ways that you can restore God's position to first place. Please give it some thought – the clock is ticking! And with God's help, you can become a better team player prayerfully ending with more wins than losses!

Prayer

Dear God, I admit that I often fall short of placing You first in my life. Please forgive me, Father and help me to do better. Teach my spouse and me how to better play the game, so that we don't foul out as much with one another. As team players, when one of us falls, let us pick each other up because we never know when it will be our turn to fall. Lord, help us not to be so defensive with each other so that we can have fewer temper tantrums and outbursts. This will lead us to a more enjoyable game. Today, we accept and understand that the "marriage game" is not always easy and that daily, we are practicing with each other to become better as we listen and follow our coaches, Jesus, God's Word, and the Holy Spirit. Help us to be productive and offer our best because forfeiting is NOT an option. Together with You, Lord, we can win! In Jesus' name, we pray. Amen!

DAY 4

Any Salt Shakers in the House?

Let your speech always be gracious, seasoned with salt, so that you may know how you ought to answer each person. (Colossians 4:6)

I walked past my daughter's room and overheard her and my youngest son talking. As a concerned mother, of course, I moved closer to the door so that I could listen in and catch more of what they were talking about. I listened intently with my ear to the door and caught a few comments being made about some negative social media remarks they had just read and didn't like. They continued talking and jeering, and I entered the room with a smile on my face. Planning to use this moment as a teaching one, I walked in joking with them, saying "So what happened?" In return, they started laughing and said "Mom!" Grasping the opportunity in a jubilant manner, I slipped in a few remarks reminding them about their words and that they needed to take into consideration the importance of choosing them carefully because sometimes, doing so can prevent many fires (problems). The scripture advises us to let our words be with grace and seasoned with salt. Simply put, let them be helpful and uplifting.

No one is perfect. We all need gentle reminders of the value of our words and the need to be wise about what we say. Has someone ever hurt your feelings because of what they said? I'm confident that we have experienced this dilemma at one time or another from an outsider. But when your feelings are hurt by your spouse, it's a whole new experience. You expect encouragement and uplifting from them, not bad words. Now, it's important not to confuse hurtful words with receiving constructive criticism from our spouses.

Speaking to each other with mutual love and respect can be very profitable. There have been many times within my marriage when one of us spoke disrespectfully to the other and feelings of guilt and remorse came over the offender. This led to the disrespectful spouse asking for forgiveness from the other spouse. How you desire your spouse to address you, should be the guiding factor on how you approach him or her (Luke 6:31). Let's face it; marriage can be stressful at times with several issues, bills, children, grandchildren, work, ministry. We all need "outlets" sometimes, to just let off a little steam. It can be an ounce of cure.

I'm curious; how do you let off steam? It's just a question for you to think about. It's true what they say about a "pop bottle" when it's shaken, and shaken, and shaken. As soon as you open it, it explodes! When life shakes us and shakes us, we will soon begin to fizz on the inside. Sooner or later, we will explode! We really need to take this into consideration. Sometimes, regret may only be one word away.

Pray and find a logical and harmless way to vent when needed. Shake it off while at the same time putting your trust in God. He will do His part, but we have to do ours too. If we are honest, many times within our marriages, we do not always filter our words; we don't think before we speak. But the hope is, as you mature and your marriage matures, your words will become more gracious and seasoned with salt (gracious and profitable) as you speak to one another. Be confident in the work that Christ has started in you, and know that the work He has begun. He is faithful to complete it. Keep pursuing the wisdom of God and know without a shadow of a doubt that the Holy Spirit is able to clean up your speech and season your marriage exquisitely. To God be all the glory!

Prayer

Lord, I thank You for the Holy Spirit, and I ask that You set a guard over my mouth. Lord, keep watch over the door of my lips. Help my words to be seasoned and flavored to the taste buds of my spouse. Lord, even when we rebuke one another, help us to do so in love. Reveal to us healthy ways that we can both let off steam when needed. I understand that words do cut. For any wounds that I may have created with my words, I pray for healing, in the name of Jesus. I also pray for any mental scarring that may be lingering within us both. Lord, we pray for divine intervention and for forgiveness. Help us both to become "salt shakers," not only toward each other but also toward those with whom we come in contact, daily. We present ourselves unto You. We trust You to clean us, from the inside out. In Jesus' name, we pray. Amen.

DAY 5

God's Amazing Grace

> But he said to me, 'My grace is sufficient for you, for my power is made perfect in weakness.' Therefore I will boast all the more gladly about my weaknesses, so that Christ's power may rest on me. (2 Corinthians 12:9)

The apostle Paul helps us to understand one of the methods God uses to keep His children humble. In a world full of sin and self-exaltation, we can easily get things twisted and allow haughtiness and pride to take over. This, ultimately, brings confusion and chaos into our marriage, just like it did with Eve. When Satan tempted Eve in the garden, it was in three areas: the lust of the eyes, the lust of the flesh and the pride of life. God had already laid down the rules, conveying that they could eat of any tree in the Garden except the tree of knowledge of good and evil. However, Eve chose to go against God's will; she went beyond the boundaries that were given, resulting in a great sin.

Isn't God's grace amazing! Over and over again, He continues to forgive us, strengthen us and help us to become more mature in the faith. With all the temptation that surrounds us daily, without God's help, power, and strength, we all would be destined to fail. You know, it truly is by God's amazing grace that many marriages have survived and succeeded this far.

Paul tells us that when we are weak, God's power gives us the strength to go on. It is His power that helps us continue when we want to quit. His power that touches our hearts to forgive when we don't want to forgive. Finally, it is His power that helps us not to yield to temptation when our flesh really wants to. Lord, thank You for your amazing grace! Today, we glory and boast in Your power; we are made better because of You, God. We confess that it was You, and You alone who did it!

Prayer

Thank You, Lord, that Your grace is sufficient and that Your power works best when we are weak. Thank You, Lord, that we don't have to pretend to always have it together; we can boast that we are weak within ourselves and strong in You. Thank You for helping us both stay humble and submissive to Your will. Lord, when we are faced with temptations, empower us with more of Your grace to walk away from them. However, if we slip and fall, thank You for picking us up and extending Your pardoning grace to us. In Jesus' name, I pray. Amen!

DAY 6

The Same Jesus

Jesus Christ is the same yesterday and today and forever. (Hebrews 13:8)

We live in a world full of changes. Our choices change, the season's change, over time our physical appearances change, our hair styles change, fashion trends change, our desires change, our mindsets change, our moods change, and even our locations may change. Yes, we live in a world that constantly changes and marriage is no exception. When a man and a woman are united in marriage, one should expect and anticipate change! You two are no longer two but one. Me should be exchanged for we; his, hers, and mine should become ours. Yes, building or maintaining a strong, healthy marriage is going to require for each spouse to sacrifice and make many changes. Sometimes, change can be scary. I mean, we tend to get used to doing things the same way for many years and change can be hard. What's even worse is when someone that we love or admire all of sudden changes towards us after years of knowing them. Let's face it… people will change.

However, according to scripture in Hebrews, the Word of God reassures us that Jesus Christ never changes. He is the same yesterday, today, and forever. Jesus is the same. He cannot change. Jesus Christ came to offer salvation to everyone that place their faith in Him. I'm so glad that no matter what I do or don't do, He doesn't change His love towards me. He is teaching me to be the same way with my spouse. No matter how much you think that your spouse has changed or is changing we are to love them the same. You have to admit that you and your spouse have gone through some changes during the course of your marriage. However, your love for one another shouldn't.

That's why Jesus needs to be the very foundation of your marriage. Just like the foundation of the house needs to be solid, sturdy, and unchangeable, we need to have the foundation of our marriages built upon that unchangeable and unmovable Rock who doesn't change with the times.

We live in a time in which the government, which includes the executive, legislative and judicial branches want to define marriage. But, marriage was defined in the beginning by God and He has not changed His mind about marriage. So, today, in an ever-changing world, please make sure that your marriage is anchored in the unchangeable God who will keep you and your marriage during changing times.

Your spouse might have changed to the point at which you feel like giving up, walking out and calling it quits but please look unto "the same Jesus" – The One who was there in the beginning. He promised to never leave you nor forsake you. He has been there in the good times and the bad. So, right now, look unto the hills from where all of our help comes from. All our help comes from the Lord who made the heavens and the earth.

Prayer

Will you pray with me? Father, it's in the name of Jesus that we come to You. Jesus was there in the beginning. Your word says that all things were made by Him and without Him was not anything made that was made. So, I come to You, right now, in an ever-changing world. I realize that some things have changed in my marriage that have me concerned. But Lord, I feel as though I'm about to go off the edge. Please Father, The unchangeable God, work everything out in my marriage. You said that if I seek You first and Your kingdom that You would add all things unto me. So, I come seeking Your help in my marriage. Restore, renew, and revitalize my marriage. In Jesus name, I pray. Amen.

DAY 7

What Does It Cost?

> Suppose one of you wants to build a tower. Won't you first sit down and estimate the cost to see if you have enough money to complete it? (Luke 14:28)

Years ago, after moving into our home, daily, we would look out our window at the house across the street from us, wondering when the owners would finish building. It seemed like the house was just left abandoned. Workers would drift in and out to do little jobs, here and there. However, there was still a lot of work left to be done. As we anxiously waited to meet our new neighbors, we would keep an eye on the home, hoping no one would vandalize it. After three years, and there was still no progress, as concerned neighbors, we wondered what was holding up the building process, and if everything and everyone was OK.

Finally, after five years, to our surprise, a few workers showed up at the site. We took the opportunity to go over and chat with the builder. "Yeah, it looks like you guys are getting close," said Blake. "Well not really, said the builder, the owner is facing quite a bit of financial problems. So I'm not sure when he's going to be able to finish."

For this owner, cost was the issue. When a person doesn't take the time to analyze the cost of building, the project could be left uncompleted, just like a marriage.

Marriages cost, and I am not only speaking of money. Marriages cost time, sacrifice, patience, understanding, commitment, loyalty, heartache, pain, tears, compromise, humility, energy, and so much more. Often, couples have no idea exactly what's required to build healthy marriages; I know we didn't.

Let's look at Jesus because He is our perfect example. You have already read in chapter nine just how much Jesus loves His bride, the church. Jesus, the Son of God, willingly gave up His life for His bride. The Bible records at one point in the Garden of Gethsemane that when Jesus was preparing to suffer, He knelt down and prayed, "Father, if You are willing, take this cup from Me; yet not My will, but Yours be done" (Luke 22:42).

In our marriages, there will be many times it will be beneficial to yield to our spouses, just like Jesus yielded to the Father. You may have to endure some things and do what you don't feel like doing. On other occasions, you will have to give when you barely have enough for yourself. Finally, it may also mean not doing some of the things you're accustomed doing for the welfare and health of your marriage.

Have you counted the cost of marriage? Will you be like Jesus and lay it all down for your bride or your husband? Are you ready to begin or restart the building process in your marriage, this time determined to go all the way? Yes, I believe you are.

Prayer

Lord Jesus, thank You for laying down Your life for me. Thank You, Lord! I confess, daily, that I fall short of my commitment to You, and to my spouse; please forgive me, Lord. I am now starting to understand the "cost." Right now, in Jesus' name, I call upon You to help me lay each and every brick. Lord, I confess that I am spiritually "bankrupt," and I am not able to build this marriage on my own. The cost is so great. I am admitting that I will need to make many withdrawals from You during our renovation and rebuilding process. I first would like to withdraw some hope to get me started. Later, through prayer, I'll be back to withdraw much, much more. Thank You, Lord. In Jesus' name, I pray. Amen.

DAY 8

Just Because

So we cared for you. Because we loved you so much, we were delighted to share with you not only the gospel of God but our lives as well. (1 Thessalonians 2:8)

As Judy pulls up to work and heads to her office, she quickly notices that all her co-workers are gathered around her desk. She looks on intently, contemplating the worst. Judy quickly changes her pace, now, walking slowly to her office. While perusing the corridors of the building and wondering what in the world is going on? Judy finally enters her office.

"Good morning Mrs. Judy!" blurts out all her co-workers.

"Good morning everyone," said Judy. "Is there something wrong?"

"No, nothing is wrong Mrs. Judy, everything is perrrfect!!" said one of the workers who then walked away.

In a soft voice, Judy said, "Will someone please tell me what in the world is going on?"

"SURPRISE!" everyone yelled.

"Surprise?" said Judy. "What's the surprise?" she asked looking perplexed.

"Here you are, Mrs. Judy," said one of the workers handing her a gift box.

"For me?" She shrugged her shoulders. "But why?" responded Judy. "Aww, you bought me a gift?" Judy held the beautiful velvet box in her hand and opened it. With tears streaming down her face, she placed her hand over her heart and muttered: "Ttthank you everyone! But again. I ask you all, why?"

Everyone blows her a kiss and in unison softly says, "Just because!"

Who doesn't like to receive gifts? Gifts are so special, especially when given from the heart. We all desire to feel special or appreciated. When someone validates us or encourages us with a gift, it just tends to carry an extra special meaning.

When was the last time you surprised your spouse with an unexpected gift? For men, it doesn't require a whole lot; you can just put a bow on yourself (smile). But in all seriousness, the thought of your spouse taking the time to do something nice to appreciate you, to express his or her love and to show you care and attention, can truly make a world of difference in your marriage. Purpose in your heart how you can express love and appreciation for your spouse, surprising them with something "just because."

Prayer

Father, in the name of Jesus, I thank You for Your many kind acts. Lord, I thank You for always doing things for me, "just because." This morning, You woke me up "just because." Lord, You gave me food "just because," and You even allowed me to breathe and walk today "just because." You are good – "just because" You are God. I better understand that it's not because I always deserve it or that I am worthy of it, but it's "just because." Lord, help me, and my spouse to appreciate Your love and then to lavish that love on each other, "just because." Bring a greater awareness to the little things done in love, so that we may genuinely express our appreciation for one another. Again, thank You, Lord. We praise You for helping us to tear down ungratefulness and taking each other for granted. In Jesus' name, we pray. Amen.

DAY 9

God's Got This

The LORD himself goes before you and will be with you; he will never leave you nor forsake you. Do not be afraid; do not be discouraged. (Deuteronomy 31:8)

It's around 10:45 PM and the phone rings, "Mom!" yells my daughter on the phone crying uncontrollably and shaking.

"What's wrong baby," I asked.

"Someone just ran me off the road!"

"What did you say, baby? I can't understand you," I said, trying to calm her with my tone of voice. "Kim, I can't understand you."

"Mom!" said Kim, "Someone just ran me off the road. My car spun around, and now it's hard to turn the wheel."

"OK, baby, where are you?"

"My car just spun around into oncoming traffic, and I'm trying, (sniffling) I'm trying to drive to work, but my steering wheel is very hard to turn!" "MOM!!"

"OK," I said. "What is the address to your job!? Text it to me."

"OK!" said Kim. Immediately, I went into the basement and asked my son, Brent, to ride with me so that we could go check on Kim. We started down the snow covered highway, following the navigation on OnStar. We slowly pulled into the parking lot of Kim's workplace, looking for her car.

"There it is Mom," said Brent. "Right there."

"OK!" I said, pulling up next to it.

Brent and I both got out of the car and noticed only a few scratches on her bumper. Kim was already inside the building so as we proceeded to go in, I texted her to let her know we were there. Soon, she came walking down the hall, and I asked her if she was OK.

"Yes, I'm OK! I can't believe that lady ran me off the road!"

"Well, the important thing is that you're OK and the car only has a few scratches. God is good, girl!" I said.

"Yep mom, I am thankful!"

The Devil is on a mission to kill, steal, and destroy, but thank God He's got us covered. "God's got this."

Many times in our marriages the unexpected happens, leaving us crying, mad, frustrated, and afraid, just like my daughter. As we roll through life, one minute everything is fine, the next, everything can drastically change. We just never know when the plans of God, or our own choices, will instantly change our direction. However, be comforted knowing that even though life takes us by surprise, nothing can ever surprise our God.

Prayer

Heavenly Father, I come before You in the name of Jesus. Lord, I ask that you would touch us right now in Jesus' name. Lord, whatever has happened in this marriage that has left us badly shaken, I ask that You will calm the raging sea. Provide peace, wisdom, and direction to both of us. Lord, only You know what is needed and only You can provide it. In Jesus' name, I pray. Amen.

DAY 10

God's Purpose

And we know that in all things God works for the good of those who love him, who have been called according to his purpose. (Romans 8:28)

As the movers arrived at the house, they looked around at the many boxes, never anticipating this much stuff to be transported.

"Wow!" said James, one of the movers. "This is a lot of stuff; we will never finish moving all this furniture and transporting these boxes within the time frame given to us—"

Before James could finish his last sentence, another moving truck slowly pulled up next to them with movers offering their assistance. Their client down the street had postponed the move and they hoped to make some extra money.

"What's your price?" yelled James, the 1st mover.

"Well for your cousin, it's free!" answered Tim, the 2nd mover.

"Tim is that you?" asked James.

"Yep! It's me, Tim!"

Tim parked the truck and walked toward his cousin who was standing in the front yard. James met Tim half way, and they embraced each other with a big hug.

"Wow, Tim! I haven't seen you in years, what have you been up to?" asked James.

"Well, man, I recently lost my job so I started my own moving company to try and make ends meet. So far cousin, it's going really well!" said Tim (the 2nd mover).

"Yeah, my client down the street took sick, so he postponed our moving job until next week. So, cousin, if you need any help, here I am," said Tim.

"Thank you man," said James, "I sure do!"

The Footprints in the Sand by Mary Stevenson is an ever popular, beautiful poem of how one person felt during one of the roughest times in life. In the poem, the person is dreaming of walking along the beach with the Lord, seeing different parts of her life flash before her. And as she sees different scenes, taking notice of only one set of footprints during the most troubling times of her life, she asked the Lord why He had abandoned her during the tough times. The Lord responded that the reason she could only see one set of footsteps was because it was then that He carried her.

In life, sometimes we feel like God has abandoned us or that there is just too much for us to "carry alone." We feel like the movers in our story. James was overwhelmed and thought that his task was going to be nearly impossible to complete. However, God sent help at just the right time; He had a plan. The Lord is not slack concerning His promises (2 Peter 3:9). He is faithful to do everything that He said He will do, and sometimes, even more. In our humanness, we can be very stubborn and strong willed on occasions, totally overlooking or unwilling to face the fact that we need help, that we can't carry life's heavy load alone. Jesus, our Lord, is there to help us, every step of the way. He promised to never leave us.

Do you have some things that need to be moved in your marriage? Some things that need to be boxed up and thrown out? Maybe, some other things that need to be pulled out of storage and put to use once again. Don't fret if things are scattered, and it looks a total mess. Jesus can help you both get them arranged correctly. He is a God of order. Will you embrace the help that is being sent to you? The job really *is* too big to handle alone. He has some of His best workers strategically positioned and ready to show up at the right time to help. With God as your helper, He can work all things together for good.

Prayer

Father God, in the name of Jesus, please forgive me of my sins. Lord, through faith, I thank You that all things are working together for good in my life, and in my marriage. Lord, I confess that I can't carry this load by myself anymore, and I desperately need Your help. Please, Lord, show me how to organize the mess, and please give me the wisdom to do it Your way. I now realize that I have boxed up my emotions, and I have become so fragile in life. Lord, I sometimes feel like a taped up box, taped up from all the hurts, wounds, pains, dishonesty, and deceit. Right now, Lord, I am crying out to You for help. Please help me to break free from it all! Help me to take each one of these boxes off my shoulders, one by one. Release me from the pain and turmoil caused in my marriage. Restore my relationship with You. Restore my life and please restore my marriage. In Jesus' name, I pray. Amen.

DAY 11

Stay in your lane

But in any case each one of you should continue to live the way God has given you to live—the way you were when God called you. This is a rule I make in all the churches. (1 Corinthians 7:17 NCV)

Beep! Beep! honks the car in front of me. "Stay in your lane!!!" shouts the driver to the car that's next to him and then speeds off angry and upset.

More than likely, we have all experienced this scenario while driving. We have either mistakenly swerved out of our lane or someone else did, causing us to respond either appropriately or inappropriately. The point is, after the mistake was committed, both of the people involved chose how they would react.

After being married for over 25 years, I can truly attest to "getting out of my lane" many times with my husband. It has only been within the past few years that I have really been convicted when I do it. That is the result of spiritual growth. I began to really seek God for order in my life and marriage through the scriptures and everyday life mistakes. The Holy Spirit has been teaching me to "stay in my lane." I am now trying to give my husband the utmost respect because he always respects me. And as we have already read, God loves order. He can teach us how to apply that godly principle of order in every area of our lives. Christ is the head, my husband is under Christ, and I am under the authority of my husband. For me, that's refreshing because I'd rather God deal with him on out of order family issues than me. I'd rather for God to deal with him than for me to try to "Get him in his lane."

Prayer

Dear heavenly Father, please forgive me for not staying in my lane. First, I confess that I overstep my boundaries with You, often, and secondly, with my spouse. Lord, help me to surrender to You and to follow the marriage order so I won't be guilty of being out of order. Normally, things that are "out of order" don't work properly. I strongly desire for my marriage to work and function in the order that You designed and intended it to. Thank You for convicting me when I "get out of my lane." I realize that even in real life while driving in traffic and I swerve out of my lane, it can be very dangerous. The same principle holds true within marriages. When I step out of my boundaries or "I am getting out of my lane," I risk colliding with my husband, which in return, can bring about confusion or some scathing words that will leave a dent in our relationship. Lord, I thank You that under Your guidance, I am fully covered from all accidents within the marriage. It's not that we won't have any, but we have a warranty, a promise from You through Your Word. Lord, You have the best policy plan for our marriage protection. If we would only yield to it, I know things could be better. The commercial says that I am safe with Allstate, but Lord, I'd rather be safe with You! In Jesus' name, I pray. Amen.

DAY 12

The Workout!

> Therefore, my dear friends, as you have always obeyed--not only in my presence, but now much more in my absence--continue to work out your salvation with fear and trembling. (Philippians 2:12)

It's 5:00 AM and a brand new day. Even though it's morning, it's still somewhat dark outside as my son Brendon rolls out of bed, legs tired and muscles still sore from his daily regimen of working out. Brendon wakes up earlier so that he can get to the gym to do his cardio workout before he goes to work at 6:30 AM. He's tired and achy but he is completely focused on his upcoming physique building competition that just happens to be in a couple of weeks. Brendon is on the grind. After his workout, he showers and heads to work, putting in a full eight- to ten-hour shift. When work is done, Brendon goes back to the gym for another two to three hours to perfect his pecks, abs, arms, and shoulders. It seems like a never ending cycle.

The apostle Paul states:

> Wherefore, my beloved, as ye have always obeyed, not as in my presence only, but now much more in my absence, work out your own salvation with fear and trembling. (Philippians 2:12)

The Greek verb rendered "work out" means "to continually work to bring something to completion or to fruition."

There is nothing that you can do, my friend, to earn salvation. However, because you are saved, you have work to do in the sanctification process. The Holy Spirit works in you to become more and more like Christ. That sounds like it's going to take some work. The same is true in our marriages. It's going to take some work.

A person who sits around and eats all the time without exercising is going to gain lots of weight and possibly, they may even experience some health problems. Now, let's relate that to our marriages. Take a moment to evaluate your marriage. Have you both been working out? Can you recall many of the things that you did for your spouse before you two got married? Did you go out of your way to do something special for them? Husbands, have you complimented your wives on how beautiful they are? Wives, have you said any encouraging words to your husbands lately? When was the last time you woke up early to make your husband breakfast before he goes to work?

My point is that marriage requires work! As I reflect upon my son's dedication to working out and keeping fit, I understand his many defined muscles and having everything in its proper place required a lot of hard work and commitment. That's how he got the results. As married couples, we too need to make sure that our marriages are fit and that we have built muscles in our relationship with one another so we can endure.

Prayer

Dear heavenly Father, please forgive me of my sins in Jesus' name. Lord, our marriage covenant workout has laxed. Our passion is somewhat flabby, and our will to do things for each other has become lazy. Lord, renew our zeal for one another in Jesus' name. Give us the stamina that we need to "work out" doing those things that seem so little, but truly make a big difference within our marriage. Give us the energy, the will, and the creativity to be dedicated to our daily workout with one another and more importantly with You! In Jesus' name, I pray. Amen.

DAY 13

An Open Mind

Live in harmony with each other. Don't be too proud to enjoy the company of ordinary people. And don't think you know it all! (Romans 12:16)

One Sunday morning, Susan decided to visit her uncle's church. After she arrived, she went in and found a seat close to the front just a few pews behind some kids. Susan sat down and took off her coat. She immediately joined in with the choir, clapping her hands and humming along. As she listened enthusiastically, she couldn't help but notice some children a few rows up, singing along and imitating the choir's every move. She thought "Wow! those kids really sound good; their harmony is wonderful!" But that wasn't all. Shortly after the choir was finished, the children pulled out pens and paper to take notes of the sermon while sitting and listening attentively to the preacher. Susan continued to stare with amazement, she couldn't help but hear the kids responding to the minister with soft voices. One of them said, "I didn't know that" and then other one said: "Shhhh, remember we have to keep our voices down and be considerate." As they continued to take notes, their little hearts and minds were wide open to be taught and their mannerisms were on point.

Isn't it wonderful how the majority of our children are capable of learning new things? At their tender ages, there is no pressure on them to feel like they have to know it all because – they don't. They are often given praise for learning new things. However, as we grow older, we allow our pride, and the few things we know to prevent us from learning new things.

Sometimes, when other people are praised for their knowledge, it sparks fear or intimidation in another person who does not know. It can also influence someone to become fearful of being ridiculed or rejected simply because of a lack of knowledge.

Well, in marriage, if the truth is told, there are a lot of things we don't know! All the pretending in the world will not miraculously make things better. As covenant couples, it's imperative that we both have teachable spirits, like those children in our story. As married couples, we both need to strive for harmony and unity, working together for a common goal – to please God. Every now and then, we will miss a note or sing off key. However, with a lot of hard work, we will both begin to tune up and take on a different sound after a while.

In the choir we talked about earlier, each and every choir member sounded melodious and in sync, but they didn't achieve those results without lots of grueling rehearsals. Our marriages are like private choirs; they need lots of rehearsals. The Director is the Holy Spirit and His desire is for us to be in harmony with Him, which will ultimately bring full harmony and strength to the marriage.

Prayer

Heavenly Father, please forgive me of my many sins, in Jesus' name. And from this point on, I ask that You help me to have a teachable spirit. Lord, when I sing out of tune (meaning I am not in agreement with God's Word) help me to find my note (to do what is right according to God). I yearn for harmony within my marriage. Please, help me and my spouse to get back in sync (to do things God's way, to pray and study Your Word). Lord, help us to exalt You and lift You up like never before. In Jesus' name, I pray. Amen.

DAY 14

Thank You

> I will give thanks to you, LORD, with all my heart; I will tell of all your wonderful deeds. (Psalm 9:1)

Lord, I thank You for my spouse; I thank You for all Your wonderful deeds done within my marriage. I come to You in faith not asking for anything, just to simply say thank You. As I look back over my life, I truly can say thank You. Lord, You are all wise and in Your wisdom, You have granted me endurance and perseverance because it hasn't always been easy. But it probably could have been a lot worse – I thank You. I thank You for life; I thank You for breath; I thank You for Your grace and forgiveness. Lord, I thank You for a home; I thank You for heat in my home; I thank You for family and friends. I thank You for providing my every need; I may not have everything I want, but You promised to supply my needs, and I truly thank You. God, I give You praise for just being God. God, I give You praise for Your Word and the promises found within Your Word. Thank You, Holy Spirit, for strengthening me during my time of weakness. Holy Spirit, thank You for counseling me and comforting me and thank You for protecting me even when I didn't know I needed protection. Thank You, God, for the many angels that helped me; many times, I wasn't even aware of their presence. Lord, thank You for guiding me, walking with me, talking with me and even at times withholding things that I prayed for in ignorance, things that could possibly have done me more harm than good. Lord, You are my joy. Lord You are my peace. Lord, You are my contentment. I say, thank You. Thank You for being my everything. You already know my desires, and I thank You for knowing what's best for me.

My marriage isn't all that I desire for it to be, but I say thank You for working not only on my spouse but on me as well. I just want to say thank You, Lord. In Jesus' name, I pray. Amen.

DAY 15

More

Now to him who is able to do immeasurably more than all we ask or imagine, according to his power that is at work within us. (Ephesians 3:20)

More, more, more!!! Life's demands can sometimes be very overwhelming.

"Mom, can I have some more potatoes, please! Oh and some more chicken too?" asked Brian.

"Sure Brian, go ahead," responded Sue.

Sue is in the kitchen serving dinner to her kids and nephew.

"Oh yeah, Auntie Sue, after we finish dinner, can we please go to the store to buy me a few more tri-fold boards for my science project? It's due in two days!"

"OK, sure, Kurt!" replied Sue to her nephew.

"Oh and Mom, I forgot to tell you that next week, I'm in a fashion show, so can we go to the mall to look for a few new out-fits? Maybe just one or two more skirts," said Sue's daughter Kim.

"Sure Kim!" said Sue.

Calling Sue from the next room is her husband.

"Sue! Sue! Honey! Can you iron my shirt and pants for work please? I'm running a little late."

"Sure babe!" said Sue to her husband.

"Oh, and we need more toilet tissue."

"OK, babe! I'll get it!"

After reading the above story, one could possibly view it in a negative way, but from God's perspective, this story is viewed in a completely positive light. As children of God, our heavenly Father implores us to petition Him for our needs and more. If we never ask God to do anything for us, how could we possibly know of His ability to do exceedingly and abundantly more than we could ask or think?

Ephesians 3:20 is Paul's doxology. In the verses written prior to this one, Paul had prayed for the saints and asked for much. The abundance of God's power was both beyond and infinite.

Wow! Now, that is most certainly good news! Let's face it; at times, the bonds of marriage can become very stressful for both spouses. Husbands and wives have to take on various responsibilities within the marriage. And because of all the stress and multiple demands that each one of them has, it's imperative for them both to take the time to seek God. As married couples, individually and collectively, we are invited to approach God's throne and to ask God for more —more wisdom, more guidance, more grace, more humility, more knowledge, more faith and more of Him.

Then, through faith, believe that God Himself is willing to open up the windows of Heaven and pour out blessings in abundance to meet our every need. The above scripture informs us that God is not limited in anything; His means are never exhausted. Not only can He do it, He can do it exceedingly and abundantly beyond measure.

God is able to bless our marriages superabundantly so that His grace and power can work in and through us for His good pleasure. As married covenant partners in Christ, we can greatly benefit from this scripture and this verse. Today, if you are willing to purpose in your heart to commit to God and to your marriage just a little bit more, God is indeed able to do the impossible.

Prayer

Lord, thank You for forgiving me of my sins, in Jesus' name. Lord, I come before Your throne of grace seeking Your face and petitioning You for more. Lord, I confess that my marriage needs more of You. In Jesus' name, I pray. Amen.

DAY 16

Remember Your Past Victories

'The LORD who rescued me from the paw of the lion and the paw of the bear will rescue me from the hand of this Philistine.' Saul said to David, 'Go, and the LORD be with you.' (1 Samuel 17:37)

Can you remember the last victory that God gave you in your marriage? Can you? What was it?

I know sometimes, it seems that remembering is so hard to do. It's as if all the bad memories linger in our minds, and the good that's been done, we suddenly get amnesia and can't remember. I recall once reading a statement, "You can do a million good things for a person, and they not even remember one. However, as soon as you make one mistake or do something bad, they act as if they cannot forget it." How true is that?

In the above scripture, David made a conscious choice to "remember." He purposely looked back in time to remember the victories the Lord had given him, to fuel and strengthen him for the battles ahead. As Christians, we are often encouraged to "count our blessings one by one, so that we see (remember) what the Lord has done." What has the Lord done for you lately? Have you chosen to recognize and praise God for the many victories of the past He has given you? Can you recall, recount, and remember God's divine interventions in your life? Or did you just think it was by coincidence or happenstance?

The Lord is with you; this is supported by Romans 8:31: "What, then, shall we say in response to these things? If God is for us, who can be against us?" My brothers and sisters in Christ, you are more than conquerors through Jesus Christ, and God is able to give you victory in this battle that you're facing. Now, understand God's perspective on victory is not like man's perspective. The Lord is more concerned about our souls and spiritual health and development than appeasing our flesh. God has a greater purpose for your life and for your marriage and when that truth (God's Word) is accepted and applied, half the battle has been won. The other half is standing and enduring the pain until change takes place.

Whatever you are battling in your marriage, ask God to help you. Ask the Holy Spirit to guide you through the Word of God and give you the strategy that's needed for your specific marital war. I don't know how intense the battle is but pray and plead the blood of Jesus over you and your spouse. Be careful of those outside the camp who often pretend to support you when they are really the enemies of your marriage.

You may need to place your marriage under spiritual quarantine until you get further instructions and assistance from the Holy Spirit. Please, don't let any intruders in. Set out to do only what God instructs you to do and do it in faith remembering what He did for you the last time.

Prayer

Lord, I remember! I remember Lord! How could I have forgotten all of my past victories? I vividly recall the many times that You helped me make it through! Lord, yes, I remember how You kept me when others left me. Yes, Lord, I remember how You comforted me when I was alone. I remember, Lord! Oh yes! I remember. How can I forget all that You have done for me? Thank You, Lord, for my past victories. Lord, I thank You for my present wins that are leading me to become victorious in the future. Lord, yes! I remember, and I thank You from the bottom of my heart. Thank You for being with me and never leaving me alone. Thank You for helping me to remember because now I have the strength to go on! In Jesus' name, I pray. Amen.

DAY 17

Fresh and New

> Because of the Lord's great love we are not consumed, for his compassions never fail. They are new every morning; great is your faithfulness. (Lamentations 3:22-23)

During Israel's suffering, they were pointed to the character and goodness of God. God is indeed merciful, patient, good, compassionate, longsuffering, kind, and He is a mighty deliverer.

Today, I would like to encourage you to step out of your comfort zone and begin to seek God like never before on behalf of your marriage. Today can indeed be a fresh new start for you and your spouse. God is faithful to complete whatever He begins. Will you allow Him to begin His transforming work within you?

Just as the Israelites were pointed to God for help, I point you to God. He is a God who loves you and is able to deliver and help you make it through whatever situations you both may be facing in your marriage. For truly His compassions never fail.

Prayer

Father, I come to You, in Jesus' name, asking that You forgive me of my sins. Lord, thank You that because of Your great love, I am not consumed and Your compassion never fails. It is new every morning. I confess that I haven't been completely faithful to You, Lord, but You have always remained faithful to me. Great is Your faithfulness! Thank You for being faithful. Today, Lord, I call upon Your name, asking You to please help me and my spouse to exhibit that same compassion, patience, and kindness to each other. In Jesus' name, I pray. Amen.

DAY 18

Turn On the Light!

Your word is a lamp for my feet, a light on my path. (Psalm 119:105)

"Can someone please turn on the lights? It's dark in here!" shouted the little boy. "I don't like the darkness; it scares me!" Shaking and sweating the little boy places his hand on the wall to try to feel his way around his grandmother's home out in the countryside where there appeared to be a power outage. "Grandma!! Grandma!!! I can't see, can someone PLEASE turn the lights on?"

Not too many people like the dark. For many, it can be scary and harmful walking anyplace in the dark – even marriages. Is your marriage experiencing a "power outage?" Are you and your spouse fumbling through your marriage in the dark? You can't quite see, and you are trying your best to "feel your way through." The Bible says that Jesus is the Light – the spiritual light that illuminates our minds and helps us to see clearly. Has the light of God's Word been turned off in your marriage? You both are walking around in total oblivion, not knowing what God has said and what your godly marriage symbolizes.

Have we forgotten that Jesus is our power source and that there is no need to walk around "in the dark" because He has paid our "light bill?" The Word of God says that when light is present, darkness has to flee. Is it possible that turning the pages of God's Word can help you both to see things a lot clearer?

Are you willing to let God shine His light on your marriage so you can see things from His perspective? God's Word contains all of life's answers. He didn't leave us clueless or "in the dark" about anything.

As Christians, we simply have to call out to God and ask Him to "turn the lights on" and help us to see clearer. Light represents the knowledge of our Lord and Savior Jesus Christ; light represents wisdom and truth. Today, I implore you to "turn the light on" and begin to view your marriage from the light of God.

Prayer

Lord, I thank You that over 2,000 years ago, there was a great power outage, darkness consumed the earth when Jesus died on the cross. However, He didn't stay dead because in three days and three nights, He got up with infinite power and fixed our light issues. Because of Jesus, we no longer have to live in darkness. Lord, shine Your light of love down upon my marriage. Lord, "turn on the light" and help my spouse and me to see things from Your perspective. Jesus, we cry out to You for clarity within our marriage and within our individual roles. Lord, I thank You for paying the light bill; and I thank You for being the power source. In Jesus' name, I pray. Amen.

DAY 19

Lose to Win

For whosoever will save his life shall lose it: and whosoever will lose his life for my sake shall find it. (Matthew 16:25)

Growing up, I was always taught to win no matter what arena in life I was in. On the football field, I was always taught by my coaches to win. In the classroom, I was taught by my teachers to win. At home, I was programmed by my parents to always do my best and strive to win. In turn, I have taught my children to be competitive and always aim to win. But, has there ever been a defeat or loss in your life that caused you to mature, try harder or to be better?

In 2014, my favorite college football team, Ohio State, was able to overcome many losses. In training camp just before the season started, they lost their starting quarterback (who was a Heisman Trophy candidate) for the season due to an injury. They had to rely on a freshman quarterback to lead them through the season. Two games into the season, they lost a game to a not so good Virginia Tech team. The Ohio State team used those losses to motivate them to improve and get better.

The team improved each and every week. And, in their final game of the regular season against Michigan, their freshman quarterback who led the team to a 10 and 1 record broke his ankle. Even though they won that game, no one thought they could win their Conference Championship game and compete for a National Championship. Ohio State was able to win the National Championship with their *third* string quarterback.

Sometimes, you have to lose to win. Jesus said:

For whosoever will save his life shall lose it: and whosoever will lose his life for my sake shall find it. (Matthew 16:25)

In this scripture, Jesus was dealing with His disciples on the subject of "self-denial." You see, sometimes, pride gets in the way. We often think that it's all about ME! But when you get married, it's not all about you anymore. You will be required to make sacrifices. Every decision that you make affects you as well as your spouse. My friend, does it always have to be your way? Do you always have to be right? Do you always have to have the last word? Just remember in any game, there is always a winner and a loser. If you want to build a strong and successful marriage, you're going to have to lose sometimes to win.

Prayer

Father, I come before You, in Jesus' name, thanking You for forgiving me of my sins. Lord, I thank You that Jesus is our great example who willingly suffered loss, laying down His life and dying on the cross so that we can be declared winners in so many areas. Father, thank You for Your faithfulness. I love You and I praise You for labeling me a winner through Your Son, Jesus Christ. It's in His name that I pray. Amen.

DAY 20

For God's Glory!

Jesus, once more deeply moved, came to the tomb. It was a cave with a stone laid across the entrance. "Take away the stone," he said. "But, Lord," said Martha, the sister of the dead man, "by this time there is a bad odor, for he has been there four days." Then Jesus said, "Did I not tell you that if you believe, you will see the glory of God?" So they took away the stone. Then Jesus looked up and said, "Father, I thank you that you have heard me. I knew that you always hear me, but I said this for the benefit of the people standing here, that they may believe that you sent me." When he had said this, Jesus called in a loud voice, "Lazarus, come out!" The dead man came out, his hands and feet wrapped with strips of linen and a cloth around his face. Jesus said to them, "Take off the grave clothes and let him go." (John 11:38-44 NIV)

Married couples can be comforted and solaced in many ways by Jesus who is the "Resurrection, and the Life." Jesus has been given all power in Heaven and in the earth and by no means is there anything too hard for Him to do.

In this scripture, our Lord Jesus has taught us by His own example to call on God our Father in prayer and to draw nigh to Him as children to a father with humble reverence, yet, with holy boldness. He is listening.

As the Holy Spirit turns the light on and illuminates our minds with the truth about God's purpose, we can be confident that "God's got this" and that it will all workout for His glory because of His amazing grace.

Within our marriages, it's important not to lose hope or relinquish our faith that God is able to make things fresh and new if we just keep an open mind.

It's true that we must keep God first not last. And when we strive to stay in our lane the blessings of God will be more bountiful than ever. "Thank You, Lord."

Even in marital situations that seem to be dead – whether it is our love for each other, our sex life, the joys of oneness, laughter, fun, hope, faith or our passion. If you choose to fight for your marriage, and you are truly committed, you will succeed. Please remember your past victories and accept that building your marriage on a solid foundation will cost. Always keep in mind, "no pain, no gain" and sometimes, we have to "lose to win."

Never forget that Lazarus was thoroughly revived and returned not only to life but to good health. If God permits, Jesus can do the same for you. Your marriage can be resurrected, and God can passionately "turn up the heat" in it. However, remember, it will not be easy. In fact, it will be a strenuous "workout."

Yielding to the Spirit is required, and you must be willing to lay aside any weights and sins that could hinder your progress. Are you ready? Do you want to become a "salt shaker for the Lord" in your marriage?

The Lord loves you; His love for you is so great:

For God so loved the world that He gave His only begotten Son, that whosoever believeth in Him should not perish, but have everlasting life. (John 3:16)

Yes, Jesus died for you on the cross. His love runs deep for you. If you allow Him to lavish you with it, in turn, you can lavish that same love on your spouse. He can do it!

Our God is omniscient, omnipotent, and omnipresent. He is sovereign, and He can do whatever He wants to do "just because" He is God!

Prayer

Lord, thank You for resurrecting my marriage. Thank You for breathing on my marriage and reviving it. I accept and believe that *nothing* is impossible for You. Holy Spirit, I humbly ask for You to lead and guide me through each and every building phase. Help me to yield and help us to build according to Your blueprints for marriage. All glory belongs to You. In Jesus' name, I pray. Amen.

CITATIONS

1 Harley, Willard F. *His Needs, Her Needs: Building an Affair Proof Marriage.* Grand Rapids, MI: Revell: Willard F. Harley, Jr. Rev and expanded 1986, 1994, 2001, 2011, page 17. Print

2 Wiersbe, Warren W. *The Wiersbe Bible Commentary.* Colorado, Springs, CO: David Cook, 2007. Print. The Complete Old Testament (OT) in One Volume / Edition 1/ Commentary on Nehemiah, chapters one-three.

5 The internet/Google/Got questions.com.

9, 10 Larkin, Clarence. *Dispensational Truth by Clarence Larkin.* Glenside, PA: Rev. Clarence Larkin Est, 1920, page 76. Print

9 Scofield, C.I. Rev. D.D. *Scofield Study Bible.* New York: Oxford, 1996. Notes from Genesis, pages 6-9.

10 Gregg, Steve. Forward by Dr. Robert Clouse. *Revelation: Four Views, A Parallel Commentary.* Nashville, TN: Thomas Nelson, 1997, page 441. Print

10 MacDonald, William. *The Believers Bible Commentary.* Nashville, TN: Thomas Nelson, 1995, 1992, 1990, 1989, page 2376 chapter 19:9. Print

10 Dake, Finis. *Dakes Annotated Reference Bible.* Lawrenceville, GA: Dake Publishing. Notes on Revelation related to "bride of Christ" and "Marriage of Christ" page 312. Also "8 Proofs the Church is Now Married."

10 https://www.biblegateway.com/Bible Gateway. Dictionary of the Bible. Themes on Betrothal.

ABOUT THE AUTHORS

Blake and Melecia Scott are both born-again Christians who love the Lord. Rev. Blake is an associate minister and the Evangelism Ministry leader along with his wife, Melecia, at Canaan Baptist Church in Flint, Michigan (Rev. Charles E. Roots, Pastor). Blake and Melecia have spearheaded the Evangelism Ministry for more than fourteen years, walking the streets of their community and going door-to-door sharing the gospel of Jesus Christ. Together, they have also hosted various evangelism workshops to further equip the disciples of Christ for the call of the Great Commission found in Matthew 28:19-20.

This power-packed couple was united in holy matrimony over 25 years ago, and they are the proud parents of three.

Rev. Blake Scott has been a preacher of the gospel for more than fourteen years at Canaan Baptist Church, and he is also a Sunday school and Bible study teacher.

Melecia is an anointed motivational speaker, a mentor, a Bible study, and Sunday school teacher and an interpreter for the Deaf. She also presides as the Director of the Deaf Ministry. Her first book, *The Meeting* was published in June 2013. Her second book, *Ain't Nobody Mad Except the Devil,* was published in 2015.

Blake and Melecia often minister in dance together at various events as the husband and wife team known as *Anointed Hands.*

Mr. and Mrs. Scott have answered the call and fulfilled their desire to help teach other Christians how to build strong marriages through Jesus Christ our Lord by writing this amazing book.

AUTHOR CONTACT

www.ScottsMinistry.com
meleciascott@comcast.net

CPSIA information can be obtained
at www.ICGtesting.com
Printed in the USA
FFOW01n1902010517